My Garden Kitchen

My Garden Kitchen

Easy weekdays and slow-food weekends

Recipes and food photography **UNNA BURCH**

Lifestyle photography by Benjamin and Elise

NEW HOLLAND

Do everything with so much love in your heart that you would never want to do it any other way.

For my Gran and Grandad. I wish you were here to hold this book in your hands. x

CONTENTS

INTRODUCTION

The Forest Cantina is a small kitchen inside a rented house, nestled among native trees in a suburban setting. With eight beehives, 13 heritage breed chickens and an organic garden in our backyard, it's also the home to me (Unna) – a stay-at-home mum/self-taught cook, my self-employed builder/beekeeper husband Aaron and our boys Jah and Leo.

As an adult I was searching for 'what to do with my life' for so long, trying my hand at many different things, when the answer, my love for cooking and photography, was right under my nose this whole time. Funny how life happens and how obvious the answer seems now that I am doing it. In a nutshell, I began by sharing dinners I had made online, then I moved to blogging (www.theforestcantina.com) and it all unfolded from there to here, this book. A few years ago I would never have ever dreamed that I would be writing the introduction to my first cookbook, it's crazy! I am always taking inspiration from food lovers and bloggers, I never thought of myself as someone who would one day be the one giving that same joy to others. And now, I am 'one of them'.

Like any beginning, when I started blogging and working on this book I was looking for a voice, trying to come up with things that I should write about, cook and share. I wondered what people wanted to see from me. When I kept it simple and only included recipes that we love to eat – food I feed my family and friends, it became a joy. When I had the epiphany to actually keep it that easy, I would say to myself, "Just cook what you love to eat, don't worry about what everyone else is doing", and there became a rhythm to my cooking and photography, things clicked and it all blossomed. I am completely self-taught so as you can imagine, I've had lots of muck ups along the way. One of the things I really practiced was my plating and presentation (and I'm still working on it), I feel us home cooks make tasty food, but a lot of us lack in the presentation department. So I really started paying attention to food I would eat when out and food I would see online, in books and in magazines. I began to work on how I made my food look and with practice, my own personal style began to unfold. As each year passes and I look back on old food photos I can see a huge progression, and that's such an exciting thing to see, growth in both my cooking and creativity.

The process of this book was the biggest project I have ever completed in my life. An understatement to say that my heart is in it, I lost sleep over this book but gained satisfaction, I was a pedantic perfectionist with each page I completed. I am so proud to say that I juggled this mammoth project, with help from my husband and my parents I have to say, while being an stay at home mum. The core of what I do is for my kids and my husband. I had made a connection in my early childhood years with my grandmother, being by her side in her kitchen, that food is love. One way I show love for my family is by caring about what I feed them. Putting love into my cooking and setting an example through my food to my kids to do what makes you happy. And cooking makes me happy. I can now see so clearly in capital letters and bright lights that this is my calling. I know this because I feel most natural and happy when doing it ... a feeling that is beyond words. An intuition you get when you just KNOW something is right, it's more than just what you think in your mind, you feel it throughout your entire self. This is how I feel about food and photography. I hope my book can inspire you to find and follow your own love and dreams ... it only took me 35 years to finally figure it out (haha), so there's no looking back now! I hope I can inspire you to cook from scratch and cook some goodness from your own kitchen. One of the best things in life is cooking, sharing and eating good food.

ABOUT THE BOOK

There are over 100 of my own recipes in this book, a collection of my favourite things to cook and eat, including some very treasured recipes from within my family. Thank you to my Gran, Mum, my mother-in-law, sister-in-law, and her Mum, for contributing recipes. I wanted this book to be something that people would want to cook from regularly as well as be filled with beautiful images for inspiration. Most of the recipes use quite simple ingredients, but for the more unusual items and tips on where you can purchase these, see my pantry page at the back of the book.

Our honey, eggs and gardens: I am so blessed that my husband Aaron has so many skills that are interwoven into my love for food. As well as being a self-employed builder, he is also a beekeeper and we have eight backyard beehives with another 30 hives off site. It is such a blessing to have honey and bee products on hand. We also have 13 heritage breed chickens and I have selected each breed specifically for their egg shell colour. There is more information on both our chickens and bees on my website. We also have vegetable gardens where we love to grow our favourite varieties that are either harder to source or expensive to buy.

Supporting Fair Trade: I mention Fair Trade often through my book. I am so passionate about supporting Fair Trade and it has become a part of our lifestyle. I not only think that you get a more natural and unrefined product (that is often organic), but I love to support Fair Trade because of the people. I want people in developing countries to be paid fairly for their work. As a western woman, I want to make that connection between my products and the person on the other side of the world who provided them to me. Check out the 'Why Fair Trade?' page on my website for more information.

Supporting free-range meats: I love free range meats because of its ethics, and if we can't afford free range, we are happy to have a vegetarian meal and not eat meat at all. My husband and brother are also keen fishermen, divers and hunters and it's always a treat when they bring home food for the family.

Timing: We all have different skill levels in the kitchen; my 30 minutes could be another person's hour. So rather than promising it will be cooked within a certain time frame, I have given a rough indication of what you might expect, in my own words: "Easy as" – things that are easy and fast to make under 30 minutes, "A little bit of effort" – most of these recipes take me between 30–60 minutes, "Takes time" – These are the recipes that require a little more love and patience, and take over an hour and "Begin the day before" – Usually for marinating overnight or recipes that require setting the day before.

Photography: All the food photos were taken and styled by me. I wanted an image for every single recipe as I personally never ever cook a dish that doesn't have a picture. I like knowing what it's supposed to look like. The lifestyle images were captured by Benjamin and Elise Photography (www.benjaminandelise.com). There is also a little behind the scenes video that captured some of the making of the book that was shot and produced by Josiah at Firetale Films (www.firetaleweddings.com), it can be viewed on my blog – key word search: "video".

Ceramics: The majority of ceramics used in this book were especially custom and lovingly made for this project by Felicity at Wundaire (www.wundaire.com)

Social media and online: For more of the daily life within The Forest Cantina visit: Instagram @the_forest_cantina, Facebook / theforestcantina, my website + blog : www.theforestcantina.com

Brunch

One thing I look forward to about the weekends is that there is no rush, and brunch is the perfect ritual to celebrate time together at home. My husband looks after the kids while I fix us a cooked breakfast of some kind. Occasionally we eat out at our favourite café or even go to yum cha, which is always a treat; but quite often to save on money, we have a homemade breakfast. Something that can fuel us for a few hours while we do our weekend projects and pottering. We always have something on the go, so weekends are rarely spent relaxing, but that is exactly how we like to be ... we are movers and shakers around here! Sitting down to brunch is the moment where we can be still and plan together how we are going to divvy up the two days and find a balance between family life, to-do lists, market shopping and maybe who we can invite over for a weekend meal.

We have 13 chickens so we have fresh eggs daily. It's a pretty amazing feeling to hear the chooks from the kitchen window clucking to let us know they have just laid an egg, then collecting them while they are still warm ... there is no fresher egg than that. I also love to brew a Chemex or stove top coffee, sometimes I cook a batch of waffles for my son Jah and my husband makes fresh juice – I just love weekends and brunch food.

We also have beehives in our backyard, so weekday breakfast can be as simple as honey toast. Or you might like to try my Great Aunt's muesli recipe on page 27. Once made, it's an easy go-to breakfast with all the goodness you need to fuel your mornings.

CHICKPEA 'BAKED BEANS'

This was one of those accidental dishes – I'd usually make this with cannellini beans but I went to the cupboard one morning and didn't have any so I used a tin of chickpeas instead and I liked it so much more. It's the perfect accompaniment to any savoury breakfast. It would also be a good base to fill Hand Pies with (see page 114) – just add a few extra vegetables, some steamed cauliflower and spinach.

2 tablespoons olive oil
2 onions, diced
1 bay leaf
3 cloves garlic, crushed
400g (14oz) tin chickpeas, drained and
    rinsed
400g (14oz) tin crushed tomatoes
¼ cup water
2 tablespoons tomato paste
1 tablespoon Worcestershire sauce
1 teaspoon treacle (or use brown sugar)
1 teaspoon Dijon mustard

Serves: 4
Time: Easy as

Heat the olive oil in a large saucepan and cook the onion with a pinch of salt and the bay leaf (to help soften the onions and stop them from going brown) and cook for around 5 minutes or until translucent. Add the garlic and cook for a further 1 minute. Add the rest of the ingredients and stir to combine. Cook for 10 minutes or until the sauce is thick and glossy. Discard bay leaf, taste and season with salt and pepper. Serve.

SAGE EGGS

Because we always have eggs from our chickens and sage seems to grow all year round in our garden, this is the most cooked weekend breakfast in our house. And we don't live too far from a bakery either so there is always a trip down there to get some fresh bread to go with breakfast. Also really good with my Chickpea 'baked beans' (see recipe above).

6 free range eggs
75g (2.6oz) butter
1 large bunch of sage, about 30 leaves
    (I used both green and purple sage)
Toast to serve (I used ciabatta)

Serves: 3
Time: Easy as

Warm the butter over a medium/high heat. Once melted, add the sage and fry until just crisp. Remove a few of the sage leaves for garnish at the end. Crack the eggs into the pan. Cover and turn down to a low heat. The idea is that the eggs cook very gently in the sage butter. Cook for around 5 minutes or until the eggs are cooked to your liking. They shouldn't need salt, as the butter will be salty enough. Just season with a little pepper. Garnish with reserved sage leaves. Serve on toast.

HUEVOS RANCHEROS

I dream of eating this in Mexico one day with a delicious cacoa hot chocolate. I love nothing more than chilli and limes – and when I can squeeze those flavours into my life for breakfast, well, that's a good thing. This, to me, is weekend food – food that takes a little more time to prepare but fuels you for hours!

FOR THE BEANS

2 x 400g (14oz) tins black beans
½ red onion, finely diced
2 teaspoons cumin
2 cloves garlic, crushed
Squeeze of lime

FOR THE SALSA

½ red onion
6 ripe tomatoes
1 red jalapeño chilli (or a long red chilli, or a pinch of chilli flakes)
Squeeze of lime juice

TO SERVE

2 tablespoons oil (I used coconut oil, but any oil of your choice would be fine)
8 free range eggs
4 flour tortillas, warmed
30g (1 oz) feta, crumbled
1 large avocado, sliced
Microgreens or coriander to garnish
Lime cheeks to serve

Serves: 4
Time: A little bit of effort

For the beans: Empty the entire tin of beans (do not rinse) into a medium sized pot with the onion, cumin and garlic and season with salt and pepper. Cook over a medium/high heat until the majority of the liquid has been evaporated from the beans, stirring occasionally with a wooden spoon so it doesn't stick to the pot. Cook for around 8–10 minutes. Once cooked, squeeze over some lime juice. Stir and taste to see if it needs more salt and pepper or extra lime. Cover to keep warm and set aside.

For the salsa: Finely dice the red onion and add it to a bowl covered with water. By soaking the onion you will take the harsh onion taste away. Soak for at least 5 minutes. While the onion soaks, dice your tomatoes (as chunky or as fine as you like) and finely dice the chilli and add to a bowl. After 5 minutes, drain the onions and add to the bowl. Toss together with a squeeze of lime and season with salt and pepper. Taste to check seasoning. Set aside.

To serve: Heat the oil in a skillet over a medium/high heat and fry the eggs to your liking. I love when my eggs have runny yolks, fully cooked whites and crispy bits around the edges – sunny side up always! Put the tortillas on a plate and top with beans followed by the eggs. Put a few slices of avocado on the side, top with salsa, and crumble over some feta. Garnish with microgreens or coriander. Finish with some pepper and a squeeze of lime. (It shouldn't need salt as the feta is salty.)

EGGS MONTRÉAL

The trump card of the breakfast world for me – this is the dish I always order when we eat out at our favourite café. You can make this breakfast the way you like it by using your favourite bread – ciabatta or an English muffin, using bacon instead of salmon and leaving off the capers, or using spinach for an Eggs Florentine. In winter I use spinach in place of the asparagus. This dish really needs some sort of green to cut through the richness of the salmon, egg and hollandaise sauce.

2 bagels, split and toasted
200g (7oz) wood-roasted salmon
1 bunch asparagus, trimmed and split
 lengthwise
1 tablespoon white vinegar
4 free range eggs
Lemon and caper Hollandaise (see recipe
 below or you can use a store bought
 hollandaise)
1 teaspoon capers, chopped
Chives, finely sliced

Serves: 2
Time: Easy as

Put the bagels on a plate and flake over the salmon, discarding the skin. Set aside.

Put some ice into a large bowl, cover with cold water and set aside. Bring a medium sized pot of water to the boil. Drop in your asparagus and boil for exactly 1 minute. Scoop out (don't drain water as you will cook your eggs in it) and plunge into the ice water to retain colour and crunch.

Turn the heat down to low so there are no bubbles and add the vinegar. Crack the eggs into the pot and cook for approximately 3 minutes or until they are cooked to your liking. The cooking time depends on the freshness and size of your eggs. I use a flat potato masher to scoop out poached eggs – place eggs on top of salmon. Top with hollandaise, capers, chives and a little pepper. Serve with extra hollandaise on the side and a mug of tea.

LEMON AND CAPER HOLLANDAISE

With the addition of lemon and capers, this is a good sauce to serve with any fish – not only at breakfast time, but also with some grilled fish and salad later in the day as well. If you make it the day before you need it, the butter will reform slightly making it a thicker hollandaise.

Zest of 1 lemon
2 tablespoons lemon juice
 4 egg yolks free range
150g (5.3oz) butter, melted
1 teaspoon capers, finely chopped

Makes: 2 cups
Time: Easy as

In a food processor add the zest, juice and egg yolks and whizz up for a minute, then slowly pour in the melted butter. Taste and check for seasoning, adding salt and pepper to taste. Fold through the chopped capers. Pour into a jar (with a lid). Store in a cool place, but not the fridge – if it is in the fridge it will completely harden.

AVOCADO EGGS WITH FETA AND DUKKAH

Eggs and dukkah – BEST combination! The dukkah (see recipe below) acts like a nutty spiced seasoning to the eggs. The avocado gives this brunch dish creaminess and the feta adds saltiness; it's such a good combination of flavours and textures! If your avocados are not quite at the point of being usable, you can use sliced fresh tomato instead.

4 large free range (size 7 eggs)
4 slices ciabatta, toasted
2 small avocados
2 tablespoons dukkah
4 tablespoons crumbled feta
Microgreens (I used sorrel)
A little olive oil

Serves: 2
Time: Easy as

For perfect "4 minute eggs" take a large pot and fill with enough water to completely submerge the eggs, and bring to the boil. Once the water is at a full rolling boil, carefully place eggs in, uncovered, and boil for exactly 4 minutes. While they are cooking, get a large bowl of cold water with ice cubes in it. Once the eggs are cooked remove and place the eggs into the ice water to stop the cooking process. Leave the eggs in there while you prepare the rest of the dish.

Put the toast on a plate and spread with avocado, then sprinkle with a little pepper, the dukkah and feta. Carefully peel eggs and place each one on top. Garnish with microgreens and drizzle with olive oil. You might not need any extra salt as the dukkah and feta are season enough for me. But taste and season if you need.

DUKKAH

With an Egyptian heritage, dukkah is a condiment that is made from nuts and spices. This is my version made with flavours I love. It goes really well with bread and good olive oil. Just rip and dip some crusty bread into olive oil and then into dukkah – perfect on an antipasto board! Or use with eggs like I have.

⅔ cup hazelnuts
½ cup sunflower seeds
¼ cup white sesame seeds
¼ cup black sesame seeds
2 tablespoons coriander seeds
2 tablespoons cumin seeds
1 tablespoon fennel seeds
1 ½ teaspoons pepper
1 ½ teaspoons flaky sea salt
Pinch chilli flakes (optional)

Makes: 1 ¼ cups
Time: Easy as

Preheat oven to 180°C (350°F). Put the hazelnuts on a baking tray and roast for 5 minutes. Remove and place into a clean tea towel. Rub the nuts in the tea towel to remove as much of the skins as you can, then put the nuts into a food processor (you can use a pestle and mortar or chop by hand if you don't have a processor.)

In a dry frying pan, over a medium/high heat toast the sunflower seeds until they are browned slightly making sure you toss regularly so they don't burn. Add toasted sunflower seeds to the food processor. Then toast the sesame seeds in the same pan, and add to the processor when done. Then toast the coriander seeds, cumin seeds and fennel seeds and add to the processor. (You want the sunflower seeds, sesame seeds and spices separate as they are all different sizes and take different amounts of time to toast.) Season the mixture with the salt, pepper and chilli and pulse until everything is combined. I like to keep mine a little chunky. Store in an air tight container or jar. Keeps for months.

MOLLY'S MUESLI

Molly was my Grandmother's first cousin and they were also neighbours. Because we spent a lot of time with my Grandparents growing up, my brother and I would often visit Aunt Molly. This is seriously the best muesli I have ever made and had! Surprisingly one of my favourite things in there is the All-Bran. When toasted it has such a good texture! I have made a few slight adjustments to the original recipe – we like quite sweet muesli, if you don't, leave the sugar out and just use honey. Also, we use unrefined sugar which isn't as sweet as white sugar, so use less than suggested in the recipe if you use white sugar. If you can't find wheatgerm or All-Bran – use the same amount of something different – such as rolled oats, seeds or nuts so the quantity stays the same. I always double this recipe and make a huge batch so that it lasts longer; it also makes a wonderful homemade gift.

1 cup wheatgerm
1 cup All-Bran
1 cup chopped nuts (I used pecans and walnuts)
1 cup sunflower seeds
4 cups rolled oats

FOR THE SYRUP
½ cup honey
½ cup coconut oil
½ cup FairTrade unrefined sugar

TO ADD AT THE END
1 cup dried fruit (I used chopped apricots, dried blueberries and cranberries)
1 cup coconut (I used organic coconut chips)
½ cup goji berries (optional)

TO SERVE
Vanilla bean yoghurt
Bee pollen
Blueberries

Makes: 10 ½ cups
Time: A little bit of effort

Preheat oven to 180°C (350°F). Line two trays with baking paper and set aside. Mix the wheatgerm, All-Bran, nuts, seeds and oats and bake for 30–35 minutes. With two wooden spoons, toss twice during cooking so that it doesn't over cook on the top and in the corners especially. Remove from oven when all ingredients are golden and have a nutty, toasted smell.

In a medium sized pot, melt the honey, sugar and oil. Pour in the dry ingredients. Stir through. Add the fruit and goji berries and toss. Place the trays back into the oven but turn the oven off. I left mine in the oven until the oven went cold and then pulled out and broke apart the muesli with my fingers. Store in an airtight container.

To serve: I love serving muesli with bee pollen from our bee hives. Bee pollen is the most amazing super food and has so many health benefits, a wonderful addition to kick start the day. I also like serving the museli with milk, yoghurt and fruit. In winter time stewed rhubarb is nice instead of berries.

WAFFLES WITH BLUEBERRY BUTTER AND MAPLE SYRUP

Waffles are my son Jah's favourite and I usually make these when he has friends to sleep over – it's his favourite weekend breakfast. If you can, find a cast iron waffle iron – I found a second-hand one and it makes the best waffles compared to the non-stick newer versions. The one I have makes waffles crispy on the outside and fluffy in the centre. Also by aerating and beating the egg white gives the waffles a fluffy texture. Serve with blueberry butter and real organic maple syrup as shown, or try with banana, crispy free range bacon and maple syrup.

2 cups flour
2 teaspoons baking powder
2 teaspoons FairTrade unrefined sugar
2 cups of warm milk
2 free range eggs, separated
1 tablespoon of melted butter
a neutral flavoured cooking spray

TO SERVE
50g (2oz) butter at room temperature
1 tablespoon icing sugar (plus extra for
  dusting)
1 punnet blueberries
Real, organic maple syrup

Makes: 10–12 waffles depending
on the size of your waffle iron
Time: Easy as

Heat waffle iron. Beat the egg whites until you have soft peaks, then set aside. In a large bowl mix the milk, melted butter, and egg yolks so the sugar dissolves. Combine the flour and baking powder together and slowly fold through the wet ingredients. Don't overmix or your waffles will be tough. Fold through the egg whites carefully so you don't lose any of the air from them. Spray the waffle iron well with cooking spray. Put one cup of batter in the preheated waffle iron and cook for around 2 minutes. Repeat until all of the waffles are cooked.

For the blueberry butter: Take butter and mix in a bowl with the icing sugar. Take two thirds of the blueberries and fold through the butter crushing them with the back of a spoon so that the berries burst into the butter.

To serve: Dust waffles with a little icing sugar. Put a dollop of blueberry butter on top of the waffles followed by some of the remaining berries. Pour over the maple syrup.

Note: I freeze any leftover waffles, or make a double batch especially for the freezer. Then when Jah wants waffles he just takes from the freezer and puts them in the toaster.

Bread

I am certainly no artisan baker but I am addicted to the satisfaction I get from making my own bread.
I love how only a few simple ingredients can be turned into something completely different with just a
little care and attention.

The idea of bread making can be intimidating to some, but in this section I have a few of my recipes
that I make regularly, so they are well tested! Start off with something easy, like pizza bases – then
when you start to have more confidence, move up to something a little more complicated like brioche.
The thing with bread making is that you develop and learn a knack for it that can only come with
repetition. The skills you learn from one recipe you will take to another.

By baking your own bread you get to control it, especially in terms of ingredients. For example, you can
choose the flour you want – you might want to use organic and unbleached flour, or honey in place of
the sugar. We eat a lot of bread in our house, so making my own saves money. It is not expensive to
make, especially if you buy things like flour in bulk. Whether you are making something like a flatbread
to wrap around a filling for dinner, (there's a recipe for tortillas on page 84) or even my mother-in-law's
loaf that is perfect for breakfast. Bread is such a good skill to learn, to love and to master.

JUDY'S BREAD

This recipe and the following Breadmaker Loaf belong to my mother-in-law, Judy. The first thing I ever ate of Judy's was her homemade bread with her homemade peanut butter. Judy has been a huge inspiration to me over the years because of her love of making things from scratch and her incredible knack for gardening. Also, Judy and John (my husband's step dad) are bee keepers too, so they are especially helpful when my husband phones and asks questions about our own hives. Judy reminds me a lot of my Grandmother in the way that she makes it seem easy. All the love and effort that she puts into what she does is done without the feeling that it's a chore, but rather a pleasure. I am so thankful that I can include her beautiful and easy bread recipes in my book. This first recipe is a no knead bread tin bread that is really simple to make and delivers excellent results (this recipe is the sliced bread in the picture).

3 cups warm water
1 tablespoon honey
2 teaspoons dried yeast
2 ½ cups wholemeal flour
2 ½ cups white flour
1 ½ teaspoons salt
2 tablespoons sunflower seeds
2 tablespoons linseed seeds

Makes: 1 large loaf
Time: A little bit of effort. Takes time to prove and bake

Preheat oven to 220°C (430°F). Grease a large bread pan well with butter. (Or two smaller ones. The large bread tin I use is 10cm high and 23cm long) In a large mixing bowl whisk together the water, honey, and yeast. Put in a warm place and leave to go frothy, for about 15 minutes. Then add the wholemeal and white flour, salt and seeds and mix well. I started off with a wooden spoon and then finished off by bringing together with clean, dry hands. Put into the prepared bread tin and leave to rise in a warm spot until it has doubled in size – this will take around 1 hour.

Bake at 220°C (430°F) for 15 minutes, then reduce oven to 150°C (300°F) and bake for a further 25–30 minutes. The top should be brown and when you tap on the top of the bread it should have a hollow sound. Remove from the tin and cool on a wire rack. If you leave it in the tin, condensation will form and you will get a wet base. Best eaten the day it is made, but makes for good toasting bread the next day.

BREADMAKER LOAF

Bread makers are so convenient and easy to use, set it before you go to bed and wake to fresh bread and delicious smells. They can be expensive, but second hand ones can be relatively inexpensive. There is a special yeast to buy especially for bread makers. I have tried using regular yeast in this recipe and it doesn't turn out. Yeast is not too expensive and once opened keeps in the fridge for a few months – so I always have both on hand.

1 ½ cups warm water
1 tablespoon olive oil
1 tablespoon honey
1 ½ cups wholemeal flour
1 ½ white flour
1 teaspoon bread maker yeast
1 teaspoon salt

Makes: 1 medium size loaf
Time: Easy to put together. 4 hours to bake in the bread maker (TAKES TIME)

The one thing I was told by my mother-in-law when I first made this was to put all the ingredients into the bread maker in this order – first the water, then oil, honey, wholemeal flour, white flour, yeast, then salt. All bread makers are different but I set mine to the fastest and most basic setting which takes 4 hours. I have altered the settings before to create a darker crust or different sized loaf, but I don't think it made much of a significant difference. As with the previous recipe, once cooked remove from the tin carefully with a tea towel, if it is left in the tin for too long the condensation from the hot tin will cause the bottom of the bread to go soggy. Leave to cool before slicing for at least 30 minutes, otherwise it doesn't slice as well.

BRIOCHE

Buttery, flaky, soft and sweet, brioche is one of my all-time favourite breads. It can be a tricky one to get right – it requires a little bit of skill to nail it. The best way to do this is through practice. My first attempts at making brioche the results were heavy, now they are light and fluffy. This French dough is a definite favourite of mine and is so versatile once you have mastered it. You can use this basic recipe to make donuts (see my blog for the recipe) or bake as a loaf to slice and make into French toast. But my favourite thing to do with this dough is make buns. Use it for homemade cheeseburgers or my Pulled Pork Sliders (see recipe on page 109).

¾ cup (160ml/5.4oz) milk
1 ½ teaspoons (7g/2oz) active dry yeast
6 egg yolks
2 ⅔ cup (370g/13oz) flour
3 tablespoons (40g/1.4oz) castor sugar
150g (5.3oz) butter, at room temperature

TO FINISH
1 egg, beaten
2 tablespoons sesame seeds

Time: Takes time
Makes: 12 burger buns or
24 slider buns

Warm the milk in a small pot until it is luke warm (37°C/100°F) – I do this by touch. Once warm, pour half the milk into a bowl and set aside. Leave the remaining milk in the pot, add the yeast to it and whisk well to combine and there are no lumps of yeast left. Set aside for 10 minutes in a warm spot until the yeast is frothy. Meanwhile, beat the yolks and the remaining milk together and combine well, and then set aside.

In a stand mixer, with a dough hook attached (or you can do this step by hand) mix the flour, sugar and salt together. Make a well in the centre and pour in the yeast and the egg mixtures. Mix for around 3 minutes until you have a sticky dough that begins to look smooth. Now you want to add the butter, bit by bit until it is all incorporated. If it hasn't fully mixed in completely, you can do this by hand in the next step.

Turn out dough on a lightly floured bench and knead until the dough is smooth and elastic (around 10 minutes). You might have to add a little extra flour as you go just to stop the dough from sticking to your hands. Just add the minimal amount possible – too much extra flour added will throw off the ratio and the end result won't be fluffy when cooked.

Put the dough into a greased bowl, cover with a clean tea towel and set in a warm spot to prove until doubled in size. About 1 – 1 ½ hours. Once it has proved you can shape it how you want to use it.

Divide into 12 small balls (24 if you are making sliders) and put onto a baking paper lined tray and let them prove for 20 minutes in a warm spot, covering them loosely in plastic wrap. They may look small but they double in size when proving and then puff up in the oven too. While they are proving, preheat the oven to 180°C (350°F). After 20 minutes, brush with a beaten egg and top with sesame seeds. Bake for 16 minutes or until golden and cooked through on both top and bottom. Allow to cool on a wire rack so the heat doesn't form condensation and make the bottoms soggy.

PIZZA DOUGH

This basic dough is a staple dough that I make regularly. I have also used this dough to make flatbreads – I just roll golf ball sized amounts of dough flat, brush with melted coconut oil or olive oil and cook in a skillet over a medium/high heat until browned on one side – then flip and let it puff up. For pizzas, you can use Italian 00 flour like they do in Naples or just white flour. I have made it with wholemeal flour before, but it's not as fluffy and crispy on the bottom – it's a little heavy. I also tested this dough to see if it freezes well, and it does! So what I do now is make enough for 4 bases, use 2 for our dinner and freeze the rest in batches wrapped in plastic then stored in a freezer bag.

2 cups luke warm water
2 teaspoons active dry yeast
2 teaspoons sugar
2 tablespoons olive oil
1 teaspoon flaky sea salt
5 ½ – 6 cups flour

Make: 4 medium-sized bases
Time: Takes time / proving of dough

In a large bowl add water, yeast and sugar and whisk to combine. Set aside somewhere warm until it's foamy on top. This will take around 15–30 minutes, depending on the temperature (in winter time, when it's cooler, it always takes a little longer).

Once foamy, add the olive oil (the olive oil adds flavour and also helps it to stretch when shaping the pizza bases) and salt and mix well. Add the flour, about 4 cups to begin with, mixing with clean dry hands. Keep adding flour a little at a time until it comes together to form a rough ball. At this stage if it's a little sticky that's ok. It will look dry and rough – so now you need to knead the dough to make it elastic and smooth.

Turn the dough out onto a floured bench. Knead by pushing the dough with the heel of your hands and pulling it back with your fingers. When the dough gets sticky, dust with a little extra flour. You want to resist the urge to dump a whole lot of flour on the dough. If you add too much flour it will be stiff and hard to work and will make the cooked pizza bases dry and tough. Keep working and kneading the dough until the dough is smooth (about 7 minutes worth of kneading). To test the dough, when you push a finger into it, the dough should push back showing it is elastic.

Wash and dry your mixing bowl. Drizzle the bottom of the bowl with a little bit of the olive oil and put in the dough, flip the dough in the oil so that it is oiled top and bottom. Cover with a clean damp tea towel and leave in a warm spot until it has doubled in size. I usually leave the dough for about 1 ½ hours. If it's a warm day though, it can prove quicker. If the dough has been OVER proved, it will puff up too much when it bakes (but that's not a bad thing if you like puffy pizza!).

Once proved divide the dough into 4 portions and shape it into 4 circles. Italians use their hands by pushing from the centre out – this pushes dough to the edge giving it a natural raised crust. I use a rolling pin (forgive me any Italians reading this!) when I am in a hurry. At this stage you can use the dough immediately or you can let it prove again for another 20 minutes and then use.

See my pizza recipes on page 78 to see how I top and bake these bases.

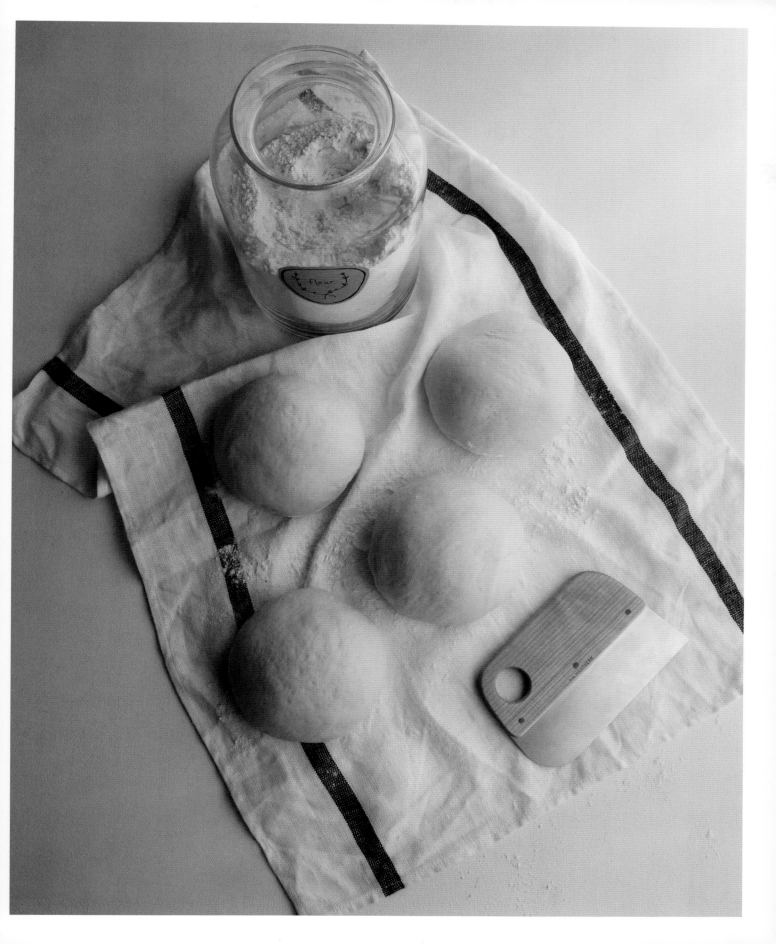

CHAPATIS

Chapatis are a no-yeast Indian flatbread that are really fun and easy to make. They are perfect with a curry to mop up all that delicious sauce! They are also great in kids lunch boxes with a tub of homemade hummus or something like that. Atta wheat flour can be found at Indian supermarkets or spice stores. If you can't source that particular flour, use half white flour and half wholemeal, or all wholemeal as an alternative. I find that the addition of white flour makes them not so heavy and a little fluffier.

2 cups Atta wheat flour
1 cup water
1 teaspoon salt
1 tablespoon ghee (or oil)
Optional:
About ¼ cup ghee to brush on each
chapati or a little melted butter.

Serves: Makes 10
Time: A little bit of effort

Mix all of the ingredients together in a bowl and combine well. Tip out onto a clean dry bench and kneed for around 8 minutes until the dough is really smooth and silky. Put the kneaded dough into a bowl and cover with a tea towel. Rest for 15 minutes to allow the gluten to relax – this will make sure the chapatis are nice and soft.

After 8 minutes, roll into a long log and cut into 10 even pieces. Roll each piece into a ball and set aside. Take a cast iron skillet or frying pan and heat over a medium heat.

I used my tortilla press to flatten out each circle into flat chapatis. I took a ball and placed it in the centre between two plastic sandwich bags and pressed flat. The plastic stops it from sticking so you can easily transfer without tearing to the pan. If you don't have a tortilla press, do the same process, just use a rolling pin to roll them flat into a circle.

Remove the plastic, spreading your hand out wide to hold and support the chapati and place into a warmed skillet to cook. Cook for around 1 minute on each side, until cooked but not too blackened. Place in a clean dry tea towel and brush a little ghee over the top if using. Keep covered.

Repeat process until all made. I flatten each chapati just as they are ready to cook. By stacking them and keeping them warm in the tea towel will keep them soft.

SPINACH FLATBREADS

If I put a bowl of spinach down in front of my kids there's no way they would happily dig in, but in these flatbreads, they love it. It's such a sneaky way of adding extra vegetables, but I'm not doing it to be shady. I added spinach because I actually love the taste of the spinach in the bread. I have tried this recipe with rocket and Swiss chard also, but I like it best when spinach is used. It has a soft delicate flavour. Use these flatbreads to rip and dip into curry or as wraps (see my my Greek Style Chicken Wraps on page 117).

2 cups luke warm water
2 teaspoons dry active yeast
2 teaspoons of honey or FairTrade
*   unrefined sugar*
6 cups tightly packed spinach (240g/8.5oz)
*   + ½ cup water*
2 teaspoons salt
2 tablespoons olive oil
7–8 cups flour + extra for dusting bench
¼ cup melted coconut oil or canola oil for
*   cooking*

Makes: 12
Time: Takes time (proving stages with the dough)

Put the lukewarm water, sugar and yeast in an extra large bowl. Whisk to combine and set in a warm spot until it gets foamy on top, this takes around 15 minutes. If it's a cold day I set it under the heat pump or put in the oven on a low temperature with the door ajar. While you wait for the yeast to develop, put the spinach and the ½ cup water in a food processor and blitz until smooth. Alternatively, chop very finely by hand and mix in a bowl with water.

Add the spinach mixture into the yeast bowl with the salt and olive oil. Add 7 cups of flour to begin with and mix well. If it's too sticky add the extra cup little by little kneading in the bowl until you have a ball of dough. Turn the dough out onto a floured bench and kneed for around 5–10 minutes or until when you push the dough with a finger it bounces back. The dough will be relatively sticky, just add enough flour as you go to make it easier to work with. But the more flour you add the tougher the flatbread will be. Having slightly sticky but soft dough, you will have light and fluffy flatbreads once cooked.

Wash out the bowl you used for the yeast. Put a little olive oil in the bottom and then the spinach dough, flip the dough in the oil so that it is now oiled on top and bottom. Cover with a clean damp tea towel and rest in a warm spot until it has doubled in size, around 1–2 hours. I quite often make my dough in the morning for that evening's dinner. I find the longer you let the dough prove (although overnight is too long) the longer the yeast has to work and it will give the bread a nicer flavour.

Once the dough has risen, cut into quarters then cut each quarter into thirds so that you have 12 even pieces. Heat a large skillet over a medium heat. I have used a regular frying pan before and the result has not been as good. A cast iron skillet gives a much better result somehow – the breads come out more like Indian naan bread with a skillet. Brush the pan with a little coconut or canola oil. Roll out a portion as flat and as round as you can get it so that it fits your size pan and place in the pan. While the underside is cooking, brush the top side with a little oil. Once it puffs up and is brown and cooked through, flip and cook the other side. Wrap in a clean tea towel. Repeat process. I usually have another one all rolled out waiting to cook. You will soon get a rhythm to cooking them all. Adjust your heat if it gets too hot and they start to burn too quickly. Stack up in the tea towel until you are ready to serve.

Dinner

I am OBSESSED with food and I love nothing more than thinking and planning what our next meal will be. For me, weekday meals are usually fuss–free and something that is easy to put together. On the weekends I cook things that take a little more effort, maybe a dessert too. Sometimes we might make an evening out of it and invite people over to share a meal with us. An example of this weekday/ weekend style of cooking for me is during the week I will use dry, store-bought pasta and make a simple sauce to go with it like my pasta puttanesca and the weekend version of that might be to make homemade pasta with a long, slow-cooked ragu to go on top. Or during the week I might use a few 'cheat' items to save on time – store bought tortillas for my tacos, saving the homemade ones for when I have more time. That for me sums up why I love food – it's adaptable and I really do love sharing these meals with family and friends. I get so much satisfaction from cooking for the people I love most and seeing the smiles on their faces when I make something they enjoy ... creating food memories, much like my Grandmother did for me. I only ate her food for 10 years before she passed away, but decades on her food is something I will never forget! I think what I remember most is not only her delicious food, but I picked up on the vibe even as a toddler that she really loved doing it. I knew that the kitchen was where she was comfortable.

Throughout this dinner section you will see images from an evening that I held for my family and friends. All the dishes served at the dinner were recipes from this book. I wanted to share a part of the making of this book, a part of the journey with the people who mean a lot to me. I believe coming together and sharing food is a celebration, a ritual people from all around the world do no matter what their culture or background is. Sharing a meal is the centre of so many strong family bonds and friendships. Our family revolves around food, it's almost in my blood to have a love for food because simply, we love to eat! I hope that some of the dishes in this section will become new favourites in your home too.

CURRY PUMPKIN SOUP

I love the combination of curry and pumpkin in soup, it gives it another level of warmth on a cold night. Soups are easy to make and if you want to make sure your soup is ready quickly, dice your pumpkin nice and small. Also, if you find that your pumpkin isn't exactly 1kg once peeled, you can also add a few carrots – I have done that many times and it is delicious.

1 kg (2.2 lb) pumpkin (weight once deseeded and skinned)
2 tablespoons olive oil
2 large onions, chopped
1 bay leaf
4 cloves garlic, chopped
1 tablespoon hot curry powder
1 teaspoon turmeric
1 litre (4 cups/32 fluid oz) chicken stock (or vegetable)
400ml (14oz) can FairTrade coconut cream

TO SERVE
¼ cup pumpkin seeds
2 tablespoon soy sauce
Fresh herbs, I used flat leaf parsley and dill

Serves: 6–8
Time: Easy as

Cut the skin off the pumpkin. Cut open and remove the seeds and stringy parts with a spoon. Dice into 1cm (½ inch) pieces. Set aside.

In a large pot on a medium/high heat, heat the olive oil and cook the onions with a pinch of salt (the salt helps them to soften and not colour). Cook for about 2 minutes until the onions are translucent but not brown.

Add the bay leaf, garlic, curry powder and turmeric and cook for a further 1 minute. Add the pumpkin and the stock, cover and bring to the boil. Cook for about 10 minutes or until a knife can go through the flesh of the pumpkin with ease.

While that is cooking, toast your pumpkin seeds in a dry frying pan on a medium/high heat. Once they start to puff and get toasted, add the soy sauce and stir until all the liquid has evaporated. Tip out onto a chopping board and roughly chop. This will give your soup a wonderful texture and flavour.

When the pumpkin is cooked, remove from the heat. Take the bay leaf out and discard. With a stick blender, blend until smooth, alternatively, pour the contents into a food processor to blend. Add half the coconut cream, reserving the remainder to spoon over top at the end. Taste the soup and season with salt and a little pepper to taste. (I season quite generously with salt – it depends on how salty your stock is.)

Ladle into bowls. Drizzle over some of the remaining coconut cream, sprinkle over the herbs and top with the pumpkin seeds.

HAM HOCK AND PEARL BARLEY SOUP

This is such a hearty bowl of warming goodness on a cold evening, it has everything in it that you need to fill your belly and get you feeling satisfied when there is a chill outside. It's a soup that my Mum made lots when I was growing up and she still makes it often. It's a great one for families as it's really economical. Leftovers freeze well.

2 tablespoons olive oil

2 large onions, diced

4 carrots, diced

2 large celery stalks, diced

8 cloves of garlic, chopped

1–2 Free range ham hocks (approx. 1kg/2.2lbs in total)

1 cup pearl barley

4 thyme sprigs, 1 small bunch of sage and 2 bay leaves tied with kitchen string (or in muslin cloth, a bouquet garni)

5 small potatoes, diced

¼ savoy cabbage, shredded

TO SERVE

Cracked pepper

Pea shoots (or parsley)

Ciabatta bread and butter

Serves: 8–10

Time: Takes time

Heat the olive oil in a large heavy bottom pot. On a medium heat, cook the onion, carrots and celery with a small pinch of salt (just to help soften the vegetables, don't add too much as the bacon hocks are very salty) and some pepper and cook for 8 minutes until soft. Add garlic, cook for 2 minutes, stirring until fragrant. Add the hock, pearl barley and the bouquet garni of herbs and bay leaves. Add enough water to cover (about 3ltr/90 fluid oz) and bring to the boil then reduce to medium low heat. Cook for 2–3 hours depending on the size of the hock, until meat is tender, topping up with more water if needed.

Remove hock, cool until it can be handled. Discard skin and bone and roughly shred meat. Set aside. Skim any excess from the top with a spoon, it's important you take the time to do this or your soup will be greasy.

Add the potatoes to the soup and cook over a medium heat for a further 15 minutes or until broth is thick and cloudy, adding more liquid if it's too thick. Add the cabbage and cook for a further 10 minutes. Taste and season if needed. Reserve a little of the ham for garnish and stir the remainder through the soup.

Divide among bowls, top with pea shoots, a little cracked pepper and some of the reserved ham.

NOTE: If the soup is too thick, add extra water. The next day if there are leftovers I always add more water as it thickens once it has sat for a while. It's also a way of stretching the meal out to go a little further.

CHICKEN STOCK

If you have a little spare time to invest in making some stock, it will not only fill your home with the most amazing aroma, but it will fill your freezer with excellent soup bases. I also use stock in risottos and stews. You can use fresh chicken frames (which are so cheap) to give you a nice clear stock, or use leftover roast chicken frames – a great way of using something that you would normally throw away, but you might need to stockpile these in your freezer until you have enough. I use this chicken stock in my Chicken Alphabet Soup (see recipe below) and Wonton Soup (see recipe page 52).

3kg (6.6 lb) – approx. 12 chicken frames
6 celery
6 large carrots
2 onions
1 leek
2 bay leaves
10 peppercorns
Small bunch parsley stalks, thyme and
    sage
6 litres (1.5 gal) water

Makes: 5 litres
Time: Takes time

Roughly chop all the vegetables and add to a pot (or divide between two pots) with the chicken frames, bay, peppercorns and herbs and water. Bring to the boil then turn the temperature right down to low. Simmer slowly for 3½ hours. Skim any fat from the top a few times during cooking to get a nice clear stock.

Once cooked, drain and discard solids. Some people like to keep it salt free. I season mine to taste as I think it's much nicer and lifts all the flavours when it's salted. Let it cool before freezing. It will keep in the fridge for 4 days and you can freeze it for up to 3 months.

CHICKEN ALPHABET SOUP

Such a comforting bowl of goodness, perfect if you're feeling under the weather. This is my youngest son Leo's favourite, he just loves it. If you can't find alphabet pasta use orzo or any small pasta. Or use spaghetti for a chicken noodle soup, about a handful, broken in half. Also if you don't have homemade chicken stock, just use some good quality store bought.

2 litres (2 quarts) chicken stock
2 large carrots, diced small
2 celery, diced small
1 onion, diced small
2 garlic cloves, crushed
2 skinless free range chicken breasts
1 ½ cups alphabet pasta
2 spring onions, sliced thinly
Parsley and thyme leaves to serve

Serves: 4
Time: Easy as

Note: If the vegetables are cut nice and small, it will cook quickly – I did a 1 cm dice.

In a large pot, bring the stock to the boil. Add the carrots, celery, onion and garlic and cook for 2 minutes. Add the pasta and cook for a further 3 minutes. (If you are using spaghetti pasta – it will need around 8 minutes cooking time as it is bigger, so I would cook that in the stock before adding the vegetables)

While the vegetables are cooking, flatten the chicken on a board by banging it out with a rolling pin between two sheets of baking paper. Dice the chicken up into bite size pieces. Add to the broth and cook for 1–2 minutes or until cooked though and still tender.

Ladle into bowls. Garnish with spring onions and herbs.

ZEA'S CHICKEN AND SWEET CORN SOUP

This is my sister-in-law's Zea's recipe (who has Chinese/Cambodian heritage) and it's a dish that she has been making for us for many years. My kids love it just as much as we do! Zea usually makes this as a starter and often makes marinated chicken wings, rice and vegetables to follow, but it's just as good on its own as a main. It's best made with fresh corn, it has such a better texture than frozen or canned and she also recommends using the best quality chicken stock you can find (or make my homemade stock on page 48).

10 fresh corn cobs
2 litres (8 cups) chicken stock
500 g (1lb) free range chicken thigh fillets
2–3 teaspoons fish sauce
2 teaspoons FairTrade unrefined sugar
½ – 1 teaspoon cracked black pepper
4 spring onions, sliced thinly diagonally
4 beaten eggs, free range

OPTIONAL CONDIMENTS
A little sesame oil or
Black (Chinkiang) vinegar

Time: Takes time
Serves: Makes approx. 16 cups

Cut the uncooked corn kernels off the cob by holding the cob by the tip and resting the base in the bottom of a large bowl (or on a clean bench if you don't have a bowl big enough – but it does make a lot of mess!) and running a large sharp knife down the corn. Be sure NOT to cut right down to the husk, so you're just cutting the top half of the kernels. Once cut, put aside 2 ½ cups of the kernels and put the remaining corn into a food processor and set aside for now.

With the back part of the knife, carefully scrape the rest of the kernels out of the husks. I did this in an up and down motion and the corn that comes out is quite wet and creamy. Once all the cobs have been scraped, transfer this to the food processor with the kernels, add 1 cup of the chicken stock, and blend until smooth to make a creamed corn. Set aside. (Note: the reason for doing this cutting technique with the corn is so that you get none of the husks in the soup. And also, so there is no wastage and you get all of the corn off the cob. You will see that the cob is completely cleaned of corn after but all those annoying bits that get stuck in your teeth are left on it).

In a large, at least 5 litre pot, bring the remaining chicken stock to the boil. In the meantime roughly cut the chicken thighs into 1 ½ cm (½ inch) pieces and add to the boiling chicken stock with the corn kernels and creamed corn mixture and stir. Bring back to the boil and cook for 2 minutes, then cover and turn down to low and simmer for 5 minutes. Add the fish sauce, sugar and cracked black pepper (you may add more of these if required) once you have the desired seasoning add the sliced spring onions (reserving a little to garnish) cover and simmer for 2 minutes longer. Skim off any scum that has come to the top and discard. Turn off the heat and slowly pour in the beaten egg (or egg whites) stirring constantly as you pour so that the egg doesn't scramble from the heat. The egg will thicken the soup slightly.

To serve, divide among bowls, top with reserved spring onion and a little extra pepper. Drizzle with sesame oil or vinegar if you wish.

WONTON SOUP

Wonton soup is one of my favourite things and is something I love to order when I eat out. Or a Tom Yum with wontons, yum! I think I actually prefer soft wontons in broth over the fried ones. These are a little fiddly to make, but if you're in the mood, once you get your rhythm, it's quite fun. There are all kinds of ways to fold these little parcels; I actually went onto YouTube to look at a few techniques. I love the combination of pork and prawn, and I also added shiitake mushrooms for extra flavour.

This recipe makes 35 and each person would need around 6–7. Any spare or extras, can be frozen. To freeze uncooked wontons, lay them on a baking sheet so they don't touch and put the baking sheet in the freezer until the wontons are frozen solid. Once frozen, the wontons can be transferred to a freezer bag for storage.

FOR THE WONTONS

1 cup dried sliced shiitake mushrooms

150g (5.5oz) raw prawns

240g (8.5oz) pork mince

1 thumb size piece of ginger, skin removed, finely grated

2 spring onions, finely sliced

1 large clove garlic, crushed ½ teaspoon white pepper

1 teaspoon salt

1 pack wonton wrappers (available from the freezer section of Asian supermarkets)

FOR THE SOUP

280g packet (10oz) Egg noodles

2 ltrs (8 cups) good quality chicken stock

4 tablespoons soy sauce

2 tablespoons rice wine vinegar

4 heads of Bok Choy, ends thinly sliced, leafy tops reserved, large ones cut in half down the middle

TO GARNISH

Fresh chilli, diced

Chilli oil or sesame oil

2 spring onions, sliced

A handful mung beans, sprouts (optional)

Serves: 5–6
Time: Takes time

Put the shiitake mushrooms in a bowl and cover with boiling water. Set aside. Remove tails from the prawns (if they are on) and chop. I didn't chop them too fine as I like to see chunks of the prawn in the wonton. Combine in a mixing bowl with the remaining ingredients. Take the mushrooms out of the water, chop finely and add to the mix and combine well. Don't throw away the mushroom water, put this in a large pot and the stock for the soup will get added to this later.

To make wontons: Wet your finger and run a little water around the edges of the wrapper. The cornflour on the wrappers and water together seal the wontons. Place a heaped teaspoon of filling in the centre of a wrapper and fold to your desired shape. It can be as simple as making a triangle, or try a more intricate shape like a "nurse's cap" or "flower bud". The main thing to make sure, no matter what shape you choose, is that it is sealed really well and there are no air pockets so water doesn't get in when they cook. When they are all done, keep in the fridge until you are ready to use.

Bring a large pot of water to the boil. Once boiling, add the egg noodles and cook for around 8 minutes or until cooked through. Drain and divide into the bottom of 6 bowls. Now add the stock to the large pot with the shiitake mushroom water, soy sauce and rice wine vinegar. Bring to the boil. Once boiling, reduce to a medium heat. Cook the wontons in batches by dropping about one third in at a time into the stock. They have to be completely covered with stock, when they are cooked they will float to the surface. They should cook for around 5–6 minutes. Add 5–6 cooked wontons per bowl. It's ok if they are sitting while the others cook – they will get refreshed at the end when the soup is ladled over.

Once the wontons are cooked, add the bok choy ends to the soup and cook for 1 minute, scoop out and add to the bowls. Cook the leaves for 30 seconds and add to the bowl. Ladle over the soup between the bowls. Top with whatever garnishes you want – a little sesame and/or chilli oil, mung beans and spring onions. If you want it a little saltier, add a dash of soy sauce.

BÒ BÚN (BEEF NOODLES)

This is my sister-in-law's Mum's recipe that was kindly given to me to share in my book because I adore this dish so much. The Taing family have a Chinese/Cambodian heritage, but cook many other dishes from surrounding countries, including this Vietnamese meal. Hao Chu is such an amazing home cook and such a beautiful person inside and out, I feel very privileged to have her recipe to pass on to you all.

FOR THE BEEF

600g (1 ½ lb) beef fillet steak*

1 tablespoon oil

2 ½ teaspoons cornflour

½ cup cold water

2 tablespoons oil

1 onion, halved & thinly sliced

2 teaspoons curry laksa paste

2 teaspoons garlic, crushed

2 teaspoons fish sauce

2 teaspoons FairTrade unrefined sugar

4 tablespoons coconut cream

NUOC MAM DRESSING

2 cups boiling water

1 cup FairTrade unrefined sugar

½ cup fish sauce

½ cup vinegar

2 tablespoons lemon juice

1 teaspoon garlic, crushed

1 small carrot, julienned

NOODLES

400g (14 oz) rice vermicelli noodles (must be medium thickness)

2 small spring onions

2 tablespoons oil

GARNISH

1 cup raw blanched peanuts

½ icburg lettuce, shredded

1 cucumber, sliced

1 small bunch mint

1 red chilli, sliced

2 cups mung bean sprouts

Serves: 4

Time: Takes time

To marinade beef: Slice beef into thin strips and place into a mixing bowl. Add ½ teaspoon salt and 1 tablespoon of oil, mix well. In a separate small bowl, mix the cornflour with 2 cups of boiling water until smooth and lump free. Add only 2 tablespoons of the cornflour mixture to the beef and mix well, reserving the rest of cornflour mix for later when cooking the beef. Pop the beef into the fridge to marinate while you prepare the rest of the meal.

For the Nuoc Mam dressing: Dissolve the sugar in the boiling water (note: I use unrefined, which isn't as sweet as refined sugar, so use less, maybe ¾ cup to begin with if you use white sugar). Add the rest of the ingredients and stir. Allow to cool before serving.

For the noodles: Bring a large pot of water to the boil and cook the noodles for 8 minutes or until al dente. Strain in a colander and run under cold water for a minute allowing them to cool completely then transferring to a large mixing bowl. Thinly slice spring onions and set aside. In a small pot heat the oil over a medium/high heat until it is hot then add the spring onions to it and while still hot, pour over the vermicelli and mix well. Set aside.

For the peanuts: Preheat oven to 180°C (350°F). Oven roast the peanuts on a tray until golden brown, around 7–8minutes, discarding any that are too dark. Once cooled, crush (I used a pestle and mortar) and set aside.

To cook the beef: Because the beef is sliced really thin, the cooking process happens very quickly so it helps to have everything prepped and within reach before you begin. Also, if you want it really hot and spicy, add more curry laksa paste, 2 tablespoons gives a nice kick! In a hot wok or deep frying pan heat the oil over a high heat. Cook the beef with the onion, garlic, curry laksa paste stirring constantly for about 1 minute. Quickly add the fish sauce and sugar, mix well for a few seconds. Pour over the remaining cornflour mixture, make sure you remix this before adding to the pan as the cornflour would have settled at the bottom, and stir constantly for only a few seconds again, so the beef will be cooked into a gravy. Finally add the coconut cream and stir well. Transfer to serving bowl.

Hao Chu serves this dish at her house with everything put into bowls in the centre of the table and everyone just helps themselves.

*you can use a cheaper cut of beef like chuck instead; the result will just be chewy.

MISO POACHED SALMON

I love this meal because it's so fast to make, it's super healthy and doesn't skimp on flavour. It has no extra salt, no sugar and no oil (apart from a tiny drop of sesame oil at the end). Kids will surprise you with miso, my son Jah loves it, from a young age he loved going for sushi and would always ask for miso soup, his favourite. This is a really quick and easy weekday meal and you can use chicken instead of salmon if salmon is too expensive.

1.5 litre (6 cups) fish or chicken stock
3 tablespoons mild miso paste*
4 x 160g (5.6oz) fillets of salmon, skin on
270g (9.5oz) packet soba noodles
2 bunches Asian greens of your choice.
   Slice stalks on an angle and set the
   leaves and flowers aside. I used Choy
   Sum because I like the yellow flowers.
200g (7oz) mushrooms, I used shitake,
   brown button and oyster mushrooms

TO SERVE

4 spring onions, sliced
Handful microgreens (I used mustard
   cress.) If you can't get microgreens, you
   could use some chopped chives, parsley
   or coriander to garnish
2 tablespoons black or white sesame
   seeds
1 long red chilli, finely sliced (optional)
A little drizzle of sesame oil to finish

Serves: 4
Time: Easy as. A little bit of effort

* Miso paste is available from Asian supermarkets. I bought mine in a tub, the mild miso variety, and it freezes well, so if you don't use it that often like me, you can freeze it for the next time you go to use it.

Take a pot or pan large enough to hold the salmon in. Add the stock and the miso. Heat on a medium/high heat until piping hot but not boiling. While that is coming up to heat, put another large pot of water on the boil for the soba noodles, no salt as they are already salty enough.

Turn stock down to medium low heat (no bubbles or movement in the stock) and add your salmon. Set a timer for 5 minutes. It will take roughly 5–7 minutes depending on the thickness of your salmon. To test whether or not it is done, press on the salmon, it should still feel soft but not raw. If you are new to cooking fish, you can take one of the salmon portions out and open the top in the thickest part with the tip of a knife to see if it's cooked. It should be slightly translucent in the centre but not completely raw, but some people like their salmon cooked all the way through, so cook to your liking. If it's not cooked, put back in for another minute. NOTE: if your stock doesn't cover the salmon, you need to ladle the stock over the tops of the fish to make sure it cooks on top, every minute or so.

Cook the soba noodles for 4 minutes. Once cooked, drain noodles and divide them between 4 bowls (I twisted mine with tongs into a little nest) they will get refreshed when the hot stock is added later. Once the salmon is cooked remove from the stock with a fish flip and set aside on a board to rest for a few minutes while you cook your vegetables.

Cook the choy sum stalks for 2 minutes in the stock. Remove with a slotted spoon and divide among the bowls. Add the mushrooms and choy sum leaves next and poach for 1 minute, then add to the bowls. Peel the skin from the salmon and place on top of the noodles and greens. Ladle the hot miso stock over everything. Garnish with the spring onions on top of the salmon then the microgreens or herbs. Sprinkle with the sesame seeds and finish with a few drops of sesame oil.

BAHN MI

When Vietnam was colonised by the French there were a lot of food crossovers and fusions beginning to happen. Bahn Mi is a street food that uses a French baguette, pâté and mayonnaise with Vietnamese flavours throughout. I had seen these on a travel programme once and had to have one! I've tried and tested this recipe many times and have finally come up with a variation of my own that I think is just right.

FOR THE PORK
800g (1 lb 12oz) free range pork fillet
1 kaffir lime leaf, very thinly sliced
1 thumb size piece of ginger, grated
5 cloves garlic, sliced
1 long red chilli, seeds in, sliced
2 tablespoons FairTrade unrefined sugar
4 tablespoons fish sauce
Canola oil for cooking

FOR THE PICKLED VEGETABLES
1 cup FairTrade unrefined sugar
1 cup rice wine vinegar
1 long cucumber
1 large carrot

FOR THE CHILLI MAYO
1 cup mayonnaise
1 tablespoon lime juice
2 tablespoons (or to taste) hot sauce, I
    used Sriracha

TO SERVE
5 small baguettes' (or 2 large ones)
50g (1.7oz) cracked pepper pâté (I prefer it
    without but it's traditional to have it)
1 small bunch or coriander and mint,
    leaves picked
1 long red chilli, sliced
Fresh lime cheeks

Serves: 5
Time: Begin the day before if possible
for marinating. A little bit of effort

In a bowl, mix the lime leaf, ginger, garlic, chilli, palm sugar and fish sauce together until the sugar dissolves. Put the pork into a bowl or snaplock bag and pour over the marinade. Marinade overnight in the fridge for maximum flavour or if you are short on time, just marinade while you prepare the rest of the ingredients. You will get a much better flavour if it marinates overnight.

For the pickled vegetables: Heat the sugar and vinegar in a small sauce pan over a medium heat stirring occasionally until the sugar dissolves. Cool completely (otherwise the vegetables will go soggy), put into the freezer if you have to. Cut the cucumber in half lengthwise and remove the seeds with a teaspoon. Cut into thin slices on an angle. Julienne the carrot. I do this with a speed peeler by peeling the carrot then stacking the peelings up on top of each other, cut the stack in half, and then cut into matchsticks. When the syrup is cold, add the carrot and the cucumber. This can be done up to a day ahead.

For the chilli mayo: Mix all of the ingredients together in a bowl. Season with salt and pepper to taste. Swirl through a little extra hot sauce once mixed.

To serve: Cut the baguettes in half and hollow out some of the bread so you can fit in more of the fillings. Spread one side generously with the chilli mayo and put a little pâté on the other side if using. Add some pickled vegetables and some herbs. Now it's time to cook the pork – I do this last so the pork is hot when served.

Heat a large skillet or frying pan on a high heat. While that is coming up to heat, slice the pork into 1cm slices. Add some canola oil and fry the pork in batches until it is all cooked, about 40 seconds on each side or until cooked through (take a slice out and test).

Add pork to the baguette. Finish with a few dollops of mayo, some extra herbs, a little red chilli. Serve with a squeeze of lime juice over top.

CHAR SUI PORK PANCAKES

This is my little twist of two dishes that I love – BBQ duck pancakes and summer rice rolls. I love the combination of the juicy grilled pork marinated in that sweet sticky char sui (Chinese BBQ sauce) with the raw crunchy vegetables. It's best to marinate the pork overnight for maximum flavour, or let it marinate while you prepare the rest of the ingredients if you are short on time. All of the unusual ingredients you might not normally keep in your pantry for the recipe below can be sourced from an Asian supermarket.

FOR THE PORK

750g (1.6 lb) free range pork fillet
1 cup char sui sauce
2 cloves garlic, roughly chopped
1 thumb size piece of ginger, roughly chopped
1 tablespoon soy sauce
1 tablespoon Shaoxing cooking wine (optional)

FOR THE CHINESE PANCAKES

4 free range eggs
1 cup tapioca flour
1 cup plain flour
1 teaspoon salt
1 ½ cups cold water
1 teaspoon sesame oil Canola oil for cooking

TO SERVE

1 jar Hoisin sauce
1 cucumber
2 large carrots
3 spring onions or Microgreens to serve (optional)

Combine the char sui, garlic, ginger, soy sauce and cooking wine with the pork in a snap lock bag. Massage well into the pork to coat. Refrigerate overnight or until you are ready to cook.

Makes: 9 (each person would need 3–4 for a main)
Time: Begin the day before for marinating. Takes time

For the pancakes: Process all of the ingredients in a food processor until well combined (or whisk until super smooth with no lumps) pour into a jug and cover. Let it sit for 30 minutes. While that is resting make you're filling.

For the filling: Cut the cucumber in half and deseed by scooping out with a teaspoon. Cut on an angle into long thin slices. Peel the carrots and julienne into match sticks. Slice the spring onions thinly on an angle. Set your fillings aside.

To make the pancakes: Heat a 22cm (8 inch) non-stick frying pan on a medium heat. When it is warm, brush with a little canola oil. Pour in ⅓ cup of batter into pan swirling gently until the liquid is set. Cook for around 1 minute, flip and cook for a further 30 seconds. The pancake should be light with no colour. Set on a plate, cover with a clean dry tea towel. Repeat process until all the batter is used stacking the pancakes and keeping covered as you go.

To cook the pork: Remove the pork fillet from the marinade and discard bag. Remove and discard any bits of garlic or ginger on the pork as these will burn and go bitter – they were there to infuse flavour while marinating so they have done their job. Slice the pork into thin 1 ½ cm slices. Heat a cast iron frying pan (I find cast iron best as you get a good hot heat to give a charred BBQ flavour – a BBQ would also work well, or just a regular frying pan if you don't have cast iron) with a little canola oil. Cook the pork slices in batches, turning, for around 5 minutes or until it is cooked all the way through but still juicy with a nice charred outside. Repeat until all cooked.

To serve: Smear a pancake with a little hoisin sauce in the centre. Add some of the vegetables and top with pork and microgreens. Fold both sides in and then roll up like a cigar. Repeat until they are all made.

BASIC TOMATO SAUCE

I make this sauce so often, I could probably do it blindfolded. It is such a staple in our house and the base to lots of my dinner dishes. It's perfect for beginner cooks or busy people because it's such a simple recipe. Make a huge batch and freeze it in portions so you have easy go-to weekday meals. Use to top pizza, use in stew or toss through some cooked pasta with parmesan, roasted pine nuts, fresh basil and olive oil.

2 large onions, finely diced
¼ cup olive oil
5 cloves garlic, crushed
1 bay leaf
2 x 400g (14oz) tins crushed tomatoes
2 heaped teaspoons tomato paste
2 teaspoons FairTrade unrefined sugar

Makes: 5 cups
Time: Easy as

Warm the olive oil over a medium heat and cook the onions with a good pinch of salt until translucent, around 7 minutes. Add the garlic, bay leaf and a pinch of pepper and cook for a further 1 minute. Add the tins of tomatoes, tomato paste and the sugar and bring to the boil. Once boiling, turn down to a medium heat and reduce until thick and glossy. About 15–20 minutes. Season to taste with salt and pepper. Once cooked, it can be stored in the fridge for around 5 days or you can freeze it.

BASIL PESTO

I love the freshness of pesto. It's so good with roast chicken, tossed through cooked pasta with some vegetables for an easy dinner or on toasted ciabatta with cheese and popped under the grill. If basil is too expensive, use half basil, half flat leaf parsley or use rocket and basil. You can also use walnut or almonds in place of pine nuts as a cheaper alternative too.

4 cups tightly packed basil leaves
1 cup grated parmesan
1 small clove garlic, chopped
½ cup roasted pine nuts
¼ cup olive oil

Makes: 1 heaped cup
Time: Easy as

Put all of the ingredients into a food processor with a good pinch of pepper and pulse until you have the texture that you like. If you don't have a food processor you can just chop everything by hand finely and mix in a bowl. Taste and season if it needs salt. Parmesan is salty so you might not need salt. To store, I keep in a jar in my fridge with a little extra olive oil on top to stop it from drying out. Use within 2 weeks.

ROAST PUMPKIN, RICOTTA AND SWISS CHARD CANNELLONI

Cannelloni can be a little tricky to fill, but it's so easy when you use lasagne sheets – just roll the filling up like a cigar. If you don't have time to make homemade pasta, you can use wonton skins, I prefer to use wonton skins over store-bought lasagne. I find the store bought lasagne too thick. The wonton skins are nice and thin and are inexpensive. They can be found in the freezer section of Asian supermarkets. Also, if you needed a shortcut for the tomato sauce, you could use a jar of store bought pasaata sauce. For this dish, I pulled some of my homemade sauce from the freezer. Always handy having it on hand.

FOR THE PUMPKIN

1 large (1.5kg/3.3lbs) pumpkin
2 tablespoons olive oil
Few knobs of butter
½ teaspoon nutmeg
1 teaspoon FairTrade unrefined sugar

FOR THE FILLING

1 large 200g (6.5oz) bunch Swiss chard or
   spinach, washed and chopped
1 tablespoon olive oil
1 red onion, finely diced
3 cloves garlic, minced
200g tub (7oz) ricotta
½ cup parmesan
zest of 1 large lemon, finely grated
1 medium bunch flat leaf parsley, chopped

TO SERVE

Fresh lasagne sheets cut into squares
   (I used 400g of 00 flour and 4 free range
   eggs) or ½ pack wonton skins
4 cups basic tomato sauce (page 66), or a
   store-bought passata sauce
1 ½ cup grated mozzarella or Colby
   cheese
30g (1oz) butter
20 sage leaves
Simple green salad on the side

Serves: 5
Time: Takes time

Preheat the oven to 200°C (390°F).

Peel and deseed the pumpkin and dice into 2cm x 2cm (0.7inch) chunks. Lay out on a tray lined with baking paper. Drizzle with oil, dot over a little butter, then sprinkle over the nutmeg, sugar and season with salt and pepper. Roast for 40 minutes until cooked and golden on the bottom. Remove and put into a large bowl, mashing up with a wooden spoon. Set aside. Reduce oven to 180°C (350°F)

Wash and roughly chop the Swiss chard leaves. In a large skillet over a high heat, cook the chard in two batches. You won't need any extra water or oil, the water left on the leaves from washing is enough to cook it in. Once cooked, add to the pumpkin. In the same skillet, reduce temperature to a medium heat. Add the olive oil and onion and cook, stirring for about a minute, then add the garlic and cook for a further minute. Add to the pumpkin with the ricotta, parmesan, lemon zest and parsley. Taste mixture and season with salt and pepper.

Prepare two medium sized baking dishes or a large roasting tray by putting half of the tomato sauce on the bottom. Set aside. Take a heaped tablespoon of mixture and place at one end of a lasagne square and roll up, placing into the dish as you go, repeating until all the mixture is used up. Make sure that the cannelloni is nice and snug so they hold each other in place. Cover with the remaining tomato sauce and top with cheese. Bake at 180°C (350°F) for 30–35 minutes or until the top is golden. Let it rest for 5 minutes when it comes out of the oven.

While the cannelloni is resting, melt the remaining butter over a medium/high heat. Fry the sage leaves until they are crispy but not burnt. Garnish the top of the cannelloni with the sage leaves. Serve with a simple green salad on the side (we had rocket with olive oil, lemon juice and a little flaky sea salt).

OVERNIGHT OXTAIL RAGU

When I was developing this recipe I cooked the ragu over night to save on time the next day when cooking for a dinner party. I found that slow cookers do a wonderful job at slow cooking meat, but the sauce doesn't get rich and thick, it's almost watery. So what I do now, once cooked, is remove the meat and put the sauce into a large skillet or fry pan and let it reduce for 30 minutes so the sauce gets glossy and thick and brings out all that flavour! Cooking meat on the bone gives you so much more flavour too. If you can't get oxtail, or if it's too expensive (as it's quite a 'fashionable' cut now) go for something like a shank steak and ask your butcher to cut it for you small enough to fit easily into a crock pot. You won't get quite the same flavour from a shank as you will the tail, but it's a great alternative.

1.5 kg (3.3 lbs) Oxtail
¼ cup flour
2 tablespoons olive oil
2 carrots, peeled and medium diced
1 large stick celery, medium diced
1 onion, medium diced
4 cloves garlic, crushed
1 bay leaf and a small bunch of thyme and
    rosemary tied with string (a bouquet
    gani)
½ cup red wine or water
2 teaspoons brown sugar
2 beef stock cubes, crumbled
2 x 400g (14oz) cans tomatoes
1 tablespoon Worcestershire sauce

TO SERVE
600g (1.3 lbs) pappardelle (see page 74 for
    my pasta recipe) or fettuccine
1 small bunch flat leaf parsley, chopped
¼ cup pine nuts, roasted
½ cup parmesan, grated
Freshly ground black pepper
Truffle oil (or good olive oil)

Combine flour with a good pinch of salt and pepper in a large bowl and toss with the oxtail pieces. Warm the olive oil over a medium/high heat. When hot, add the oxtail and cook in batches until brown. This process seals the meat and adds flavour to the finished ragu. Add the meat to a slow cooker with the remaining ingredients (except the Worcestershire sauce) and enough water to fill to the top. Turn onto the lowest setting. I put mine on at 6pm and turned it off when I woke at 7am the next morning.

Once cooked, remove the meat from the slow cooker. Discard the bouquet garni. Spoon off any fat or excess oil that has come to the surface. Pour remaining ragu ingredients into a large skillet or frying pan. You want a large open pan so the sauce reduces quickly, if it's in a small or deep pot it will take far longer to reduce. Add the Worcestershire sauce and enough salt and pepper to season to taste. Reduce for 30–40 minutes or until the sauce is thick, glossy and rich. While the sauce is reducing, and when the meat is cool enough to handle, shred the meat and discard the bone and any fatty bits. Once the sauce is reduced, add the shredded meat and fold through. (At this stage I allowed the sauce to cool and refrigerated until ready to warm again when my guests arrived later that evening)

To serve: Put a large pot of salted water on the boil and cook your pasta. Save about a cup of pasta water and then drain the pasta. Warm your meat sauce in a large skillet or pan. Once it is hot, add the pasta to the sauce with a little of the pasta water to loosen and toss through the sauce. Divide between warmed plates, top with any ragu left in the bottom of the pan. Grate over the parmesan, and scatter over pine nuts, add a little cracked pepper and flat leaf parsley. Finish with a drizzle of your best olive oil – I used truffle oil (why the heck not?)

Cooking note: Alternatively you can cook the ragu in a low, 150°C (300°F) oven for 3 ½ –4 hours or until the meat pulls from the bone with no effort. Shin will take longer than oxtail to cook.

Serves: 6
Time: Take time

HOMEMADE PASTA

Fresh pasta is one of those things that gets easier every time you make it because you start to get to know what it is supposed to look and feel like, it is similar to bread making in that way. The first time I made pasta it didn't have nearly enough 'bite' when it was cooked, and apparently that's because I didn't knead it long enough at the beginning. I'm still relativity new to pasta making but I do enjoy the process and it makes me feel like I'm doing good things when I make it.

600g 00 pasta flour*
6 large free range eggs
Large pinch flaky sea salt

Serves: 6
Time: Takes time

(General rule of thumb is 100g 00 flour and 1 free range egg per person) *Pasta flour is available from specialty stores. It is finely sieved flour used for pasta making in Italy.

I prefer to mix in a bowl, some people do it straight on the bench, but my eggs always drip everywhere and makes a big mess, so I place the measured flour inside a large bowl and make a well in the centre. Crack the eggs into the middle, add a pinch of salt and whisk with a fork. Then mix together to form a rough dough. Turn out onto the bench and knead for 10 minutes until the dough is silky and smooth. It's tiring work so I find the best way for me is to divide the dough into two portions and I "lean and press" my body weight onto my hands with a portion of dough under each hand. Cut the dough into quarters. Before chilling in the fridge and while the dough is soft, roll each of the quarters out with a rolling pin as thin as you can. Individually wrap each rolled out quarter up in plastic wrap, stack on a plate – chill for at least 1 hour. By doing this step of rolling the dough out while it's a warm soft dough makes it so much easier to initially feed through the first setting of the pasta machine. Portioning the pasta dough into quarters means you can take out one piece at a time and keep the remaining refrigerated when making your pasta.

Once the dough has chilled, you can make lasagne sheets, bows, ravioli … let your imagination run wild! You can also make spinach, beetroot and squid ink pasta to add colour and flavour when you are up to the stage of wanting to experiment a bit more. Below is how I make my favourite, Pappardelle.

For papadelle: Feed the chilled pasta sheets one at a time through the machine making the notch smaller each time. I take mine to a number 8 (second to last on machine). Dust the long sheet of pasta with 00 flour and fold in half to mark. On a board, cut in half at the mark. Fold again in half, marking by pressing gently. Open back up and cut at the mark. Layer all 4 sheets on top of each other making sure it's dusted with 00 flour between each sheet or it will stick when you cut it. At this stage you have nice large lasagne sheets. Fold up into thirds and then cut across into approx. 1.5 cm (½ inch) strips. Break pappardelle apart by lifting it up and shaking it lightly, dusting with a little extra flour. I store mine in a large rectangle plastic container, repeat the process until all the pasta has been made. I separate each quarter of pasta dough I make into pappardelle with a sheet of baking paper between them. This just prevents them all clumping together. When ready to cook (I sometimes prepare my pasta a few hours ahead of cooking it) cook in a large pot of boiling salted water for 4 minutes or until it is cooked to your liking. Serve with your favourite sauce. Or try my Overnight Oxtail Ragu on page 70.

PASTA PUTTANESCA

This is the most cooked dish in my house from this book. I make it so often I can do it without thinking – and I love that! I have such a rhythm with this recipe that it's on the table in 15 minutes – and we all need meals like that up our sleeves for "those" nights. While the pasta water is coming up to a boil I chop the ingredients, then when the pasta is cooking the sauce reduces. That's why this is the most made dish for me – it's fast and easy (Puttanesca translates to whore – which is part of the reason, the quick and easy part, that this recipe got its name … so I heard) and I always have the ingredients to make this in my pantry and fridge. Don't be discouraged by the anchovies and the capers – they are there for saltiness, and it does all work out in the end, I promise. The anchovies won't make the dish taste fishy, much like when using fish sauce in South East Asian dishes – the sauce gives the dish saltiness rather than a fishy taste. If I don't have a fresh chilli, I use a pinch of chilli flakes. If you're the sort of person who HAS to have meat with a dish, serve this with a piece of grilled chicken and top it with a dollop of pesto! Delicious.

6 anchovies in olive oil

4 cloves garlic, crushed

2 tablespoons capers, finely chopped

Zest 2 large lemons, finely chopped

1 long red chilli, finely chopped (or a
    teaspoon chilli flakes, less if you want it
    not so hot)

2 tablespoons olive oil

2x 400g (14oz) tin chopped tomatoes

2 tablespoons tomato paste

2 teaspoons FairTrade unrefined sugar

500g (1lb) spaghetti pasta

TO SERVE
Juice of 1 lemon

1 cup grated parmesan + extra to garnish

¼ cup pine nuts, toasted

Small bunch basil or flatleaf parsley

Good olive oil to finish

Serves: 4

Time: Easy as

Bring a large pot of hot water to the boil, covered. While that is coming to the boil, chop the garlic, capers, lemon zest and chilli and set aside. Once the water is boiling, salt it generously and cook pasta until al dente, around 7–8 minutes or until cooked to your liking.

While the pasta is cooking, first open the cans of tomatoes and set aside. Heat a large skillet or frying pan with olive oil over a high heat. When the oil is hot, first cook the anchovies, breaking them up with a wooden spoon as you go and melt them into the oil. Then add all at once the garlic, capers, lemon zest and chilli and cook while continuously stirring, for about 1 minute. As soon as the garlic starts to colour (you don't want it to burn or the sauce will be bitter) pour in the tinned tomatoes to stop the garlic getting any extra colour. Add the tomato paste and sugar and stir well. Let it bubble away, stirring occasionally while the pasta cooks. Don't cook the sauce in a small pot or it won't reduce in time. It needs to be in a big, open wide frying pan for it to cook quickly. Remove sauce from the heat.

Reserve a mug of pasta water before draining pasta. Add the pasta to the sauce and toss well, using two wooden spoons if you need. Add the parmesan cheese, lemon juice and some of the pasta water to loosen the pasta and the sauce, toss again. Taste and see if you need salt, pepper or more lemon juice. Divide among plates. Garnish with pine nuts, a little extra parmesan over each plate, basil or parsley leaves over top. Finish with a little pepper and a drizzle of olive oil.

PORK AND FENNEL PIZZA

Pork and fennel is such a great combination. If you can't find pork and fennel sausages add a teaspoon of toasted and ground fennel seeds to plain pork sausages instead. That squeeze of lemon over the pizza at the end just lifts all the flavours and gives a lovely freshness.

For the pizza dough (see page 36)

FOR THE PIZZA SAUCE
(makes enough for 2 pizzas)
2 tablespoons olive oil
1 large onion, finely diced
2 cloves garlic, crushed
1 x 400g (14oz) tin crushed tomatoes
2 teaspoons tomato paste
1 teaspoon unrefined sugar

FOR THE TOPPING
4 free range pork and fennel sausages
2 tablespoons olive oil
1 cup cheese, grated (I used Colby)
1 medium fennel bulb, fronds reserved for garnish
¼ cup pine nuts, toasted
Juice from 1 lemon

Makes: 2 large pizzas
Time: Takes time

For the pizza sauce, heat the olive oil in a large pot and cook the onion with a pinch of salt and pepper for 3–5minutes, stirring regularly until the onion is translucent but not brown. Add the garlic and cook for a further 1 minute, then add the tin of tomatoes, plus half a tomato can of water, the tomato paste and sugar. Increase heat to high to bring to a bubble. Once bubbling, reduce to a medium/low heat and simmer for 10 minutes until thick and glossy. Taste and season with salt and pepper, if desired. Remove and cool in a bowl. It's best if the pizza sauce is cold before adding to the pizza. You can make the pizza sauce up to 5 days ahead and keep covered in the fridge.

Preheat oven to 180°C (350°F) and have your pizza bases on baking paper lined trays ready. For the sausage balls, squeeze the sausage meat out of the casings to get little balls of meat (it's ok if they are not perfectly round) – I get around 6–7 balls per sausage. Heat a large skillet or frying pan over a high heat. Fry the sausage balls in two batches until crispy. They will cook further in the oven too so they don't need to be cooked all the way through. To assemble the pizza, spread tomato sauce over base, sprinkle over cheese and place the sausage balls over the top. Bake for 18–20 minutes or until the base is cooked through. To check, just lift the base up slightly with a knife to see if it's browned underneath. When it comes out of the oven, garnish with pine nuts and shave over fennel with a mandolin (or cut as finely as you can with a knife) When it has cooled slightly, garnish with fennel fronds. Squeeze over a little lemon juice all over the pizza. It might need a little salt and pepper seasoning to finish.

MARGARITA PIZZA

A simple classic combination of tomato, basil and cheese! My all-time favourite pizza, especially the wood fired ones. But this is a reliable homemade version. Occasionally I throw on some hot salami for good measure!

Pizza dough (see page 36)
Pizza sauce (same as previous recipe)

1 cup grated tasty cheese
Fresh basil leaves (about 30) 2–3 large fresh balls of mozzarella

Makes: 2 large pizzas
Time: Easy as

Make the pizza the same as the previous recipe by spreading the tomato sauce over the pizza bases then top with the grated cheese. Top with a few basil leaves, reserving a few to garnish at the end, and top with slices of mozzarella.

Bake at 180°C (350°F). Bake for 18–20 minutes or until the base is cooked through. Allow to cool slightly before adding the fresh basil (the basil will turn black if it's too hot). Season with a little salt and pepper and serve!

RISOTTO WITH ROASTED TOMATOES, BASIL AND WHITE TRUFFLE OIL

Once you have a basic understanding of how to make a simple risotto, you can add whatever flavour you like. Mushrooms and roasted pumpkin are some of our favourites to add. This combination I love – the tomatoes are so deep and sweet, the basil gives that herby freshness and the truffle oil that little bit of luxury. Truffle oil is not that much more expensive than a really good olive oil, you may get a smaller amount in comparison, but I only use it as a finishing oil so one bottle will last me half a year so it is well worth the investment. Sometimes I top risotto with a piece of grilled fish (reducing the amount of parmesan so it doesn't overpower the fish).

FOR THE TOMATOES
650g (1.7 lb) cherry tomatoes
1 tablespoon olive oil
1 teaspoon FairTrade unrefined sugar

FOR THE RISOTTO
4 cups stock (chicken or vegetable)
50g (1.7oz) butter
2 tablespoons olive oil
1 large onion, diced
1 ½ cups aborio rice 2 cloves garlic
1 cup white wine crushed
1 cup grated parmesan

TO SERVE
¼ cup grated parmesan
Baby basil leaves
Truffle oil to drizzle

Serves: 3–4
Time: A little bit of effort

Preheat oven to 200°C (390°F) Line a tray with baking paper and set aside.

For cherry tomatoes: Cut in half, if you have slightly bigger vine tomatoes cut into quarters. Scatter cut tomatoes over the prepared tray – give them space, if they are clustered together they tend to stew together, but when apart they turn almost semi-sundried like. Top with herbs. Drizzle with olive oil, a little salt and 1 teaspoon of sugar. Bake for 30–40 minutes or until they are 'raisin' like. Depending on the size and variety some need a little more cooking. Sometimes I cook them until they start to blacken, then turn off the oven and leave them in there to dry out the liquid around the tomatoes. When cooked and are looking like semi-sundried tomatoes, remove from oven and set aside.

For the risotto: Heat the stock and the butter so the butter melts into the stock. Keep hot but not boiling. In a large skillet or frying pan heat the olive oil over a medium/high heat. Cook the onion with a pinch of salt until it is soft and translucent, about 3 minutes, then add the rice and stir. The rice must toast and also become part translucent – continue stirring so that the onions don't over colour, for about 3 minutes. Add the garlic and cook for a further 30 seconds. Pour in the wine and turn down to a medium/low heat and cook off until the wine has fully evaporated. Then add one ladle of the hot stock, stirring and when that fully absorbs into the rice, add another ladle, stirring rice with a wooden spoon regularly. Repeat ladling in the stock and stirring until all the stock has been used. This process takes me 20 minutes. If your heat is too high the stock will cook off too quickly and the rice won't be cooked. The risotto should be loose and creamy not thick and gluggy. Once the risotto is cooked, add the parmesan and stir. Taste and see if you would like to season with additional salt or pepper. Gently fold half of the roasted tomatoes into the risotto reserving some for garnish.

To serve immediately, divide between warm plates. Top with the reserved tomatoes, a little extra grated parmesan and basil leaves. Drizzle with truffle oil and finish with a little extra pepper.

HOMEMADE TORTILLAS

Masa flour, made from corn, is from Central and Southern Mexico and wheat flour (used for burritos and quesadillas) is from the North. I am partial to the flavour of corn more than wheat and love making my own tortillas for tacos. The smell of masa flour cooking when I make these makes me dream of one day living in Mexico. There are three types of masa flour that I use, yellow, white and blue. It might be a little hard to get a hold of masa flour depending on where you live, but there are a few places online that sell it and deliver it to your door (check my pantry page at the back of the book for where I buy mine). Also, if you don't have a tortilla press, just use a rolling pin.

2 cups masa flour (I used an organic yellow masa for the tortillas pictured here)
2 tablespoons olive oil (to stop the tortillas from sticking in the skillet)
Pinch of salt
1 – 1 ¼ cup warm water

Makes: 16
Time: A little bit of effort

Mix the masa, oil and salt together in a bowl and slowly add the water, mixing with your hands to form a dough that feels like a slightly wet cookie dough. I usually know when I have the consistency right when I go to press the tortillas – if they press together well it's good, if they are too wet they will tear and rip easily, so I add more masa. If it is too dry add a little extra water. I do a test of one first by pressing it in the tortilla press. Once the dough is good, let it rest for 15 minutes.

Warm a cast iron skillet (they really are made best in a skillet) or if you don't have one, a large frying pan, on a medium heat. Divide dough into 16 portions, about the size of a golf ball. Using a tortilla press, between two bits of plastic, (I use two sandwich zip lock bags) put the tortilla in the centre of the press and flatten to a tortilla. Open up and flip the plastic and tortilla over, close and press again. (Or you can roll between plastic with a rolling pin, the plastic stops it sticking to the press).

Spread out your fingers as wide as they go to hold and support the tortilla so it doesn't rip. Peel off the bottom plastic, flip into your other hand, fingers spread wide and peel off the other plastic bag and then flip carefully so it is flat into a dry, preheated skillet to cook.

Cook for around 30 seconds, then flip and cook for 15–30 seconds, then flip back again and press down on the tortilla with a fish flip or I use a palate knife and let it puff up. Remove and keep warm and soft in a tea towel until you are ready to serve. Repeat process until all the tortillas are cooked.

FISH TACOS WITH CHIPOTLE MAYONNAISE

This is one of my all-time favourite dinners! I love baking the crumbed fish, it's much healthier than frying, and you can do a whole tray of fillets at once so it's really fast and easy when cooking for a family. Use a medium fillet of your favourite white fish, I cut the fish into 3 portions, one fillet makes 3 tacos, and 3 tacos is pretty filling for one person. So it's an economical way of making fish go a long way. I think fish tacos have to be in a soft tortilla and have a punchy mayo to go with them because there is nothing worse than a bland fish taco! The chipotles I use are the ones that come in adobo sauce (I use the La Morena brand). If you can't find Chipotles, use some of your favourite hot sauce to taste.

FOR THE CHIPOTLE MAYO

1 cup mayonnaise
3–4 Chipotle Peppers in adobo sauce
Squeeze of lime juice

FOR THE SLAW

450g (15oz) bag coleslaw (or you can cut your own)
1 medium fennel bulb
1 green apple
¼ sunflower seeds
1 teaspoon celery seeds
Lime juice
2 tablespoons olive oil

FOR THE FISH

6 medium fillets of your favourite white fish. (I like using something soft and flaky)
2 cups panko bread crumbs
2 teaspoons Mexican (or regular) dried oregano
1 teaspoon dried chilli flakes
Salt and Pepper to season
4 free range eggs
1 cup flour

TO SERVE

18 corn soft tortillas
Lime wedges
Microgreens
Diced chilli

Serves: 6
Time: Takes time

For the mayo: In a food processor blend the mayo and the chipotles (the chipotles have a bit of heat to them so use less if you don't like things hot) until smooth. Alternatively, you can cut chillies finely by hand and fold through. Add a little lime juice to taste. Season with salt and pepper if it needs it. Mix again and set aside.

For the slaw: Empty the bag of coleslaw into a large bowl. Take the tough core out of the fennel and slice as thinly as you can. I use a mandolin which is superfast! Pick the fennel fronds off and add to the slaw with the fennel. Slice the apple as thin as you can, I used the mandolin again, then stack up the pieces and cut into matchsticks. Squeeze over some lime juice to stop it from going brown and rub through gently with your fingers. Add to the bowl with the sesame and celery seeds, salt, pepper, olive oil and some lime juice. Toss gently, taste to check seasoning and set aside.

For the fish: Preheat oven to 200°C (390°F) on fan bake. Line a tray with baking paper.

The fillet has two parts – cut the smaller fillet off. The larger one, cut in half on a steep angle so that they are all approximately the same length and size so they cook evenly. Set all the prepared fillets aside. To set up the breading station, take 3 bowls or dishes and in the first one put flour, in the second, crack the eggs and whisk with a fork, and in the third mix together the breadcrumbs, oregano, chilli and season with salt and pepper. Dip the fillets into the flour, then egg, then coat well in the crumbs. Place on baking tray. Drizzle with olive oil and bake for around 8–10 minutes. In the last 4 minutes, add the tortillas to the oven to warm through. The tops of the fish might not be completely golden, but the bottoms will be, so use that side as your presentation side.

To serve: I serve everything in bowls and take the tray of fish to the table. Everyone DIY's their own tacos. Take a tortilla, add a little mayo to the bottom followed by some slaw. Top with a piece of fish, a little more mayo, some microgreens and fresh chilli if you wish and a squeeze of fresh lime.

BEEF AND BEAN NACHOS

This is my eldest son Jah's favourite. We don't have it that often, but whenever I say "Nachos for dinner" I get a "yussss!". So I have included this recipe in the book especially for him so now I can say "Hey, why don't you pull out the book and make the nachos?" (This book is going to come in handy around here!) Sometimes you want just something easy and they make perfect movie night food. Try it with blue corn chips if you can find them, they are so tasty!

2 tablespoons olive oil
1 large onion, diced
3 cloves garlic, crushed
600g (1.3 lb) minced beef
1 beef stock cube
1 tablespoon Worcestershire sauce
2 tablespoons tomato paste
1 teaspoon cumin
1 teaspoon FairTrade unrefined sugar
Pinch of all spice
1 bay leaf
1 x 400g (14oz) tin crushed tomatoes
1 x 400g (14oz) tin hot chilli beans

TO SERVE

2 large bags corn chips
1 cup grated tasty cheese
250g (8.8oz) tub sour cream
5 tablespoons cream
Guacamole (see recipe below)
Black sesame seeds
Coriander

Serves: 4   Time: A little bit of effort

Heat a large frying pan on a medium heat with the olive oil. Cook the onions with a pinch of salt until translucent, around 5 minutes. Add the garlic and cook for a further 1 minute. Turn the heat up to high and add the beef, breaking up as it cooks until it has browned. Crumble over the beef stock cube, add the tomato paste, Worcestershire sauce, cumin, all spice and sugar and stir to combine. Add the bay leaf, tin tomatoes, and chilli beans, stir well and let it reduce over a medium heat for around 20 minutes or until most of the liquid has absorbed and the sauce is thick and glossy. When done, discard the bay leaf. Taste and season with salt and pepper. NOTE: When the beef and bean mixture has almost finished cooking, preheat the grill in the oven to melt the cheese.

To serve: Put your corn chips on a plate and spoon over some of the beef and bean mixture. Add the cheese on top then pop under the grill to melt. While that is melting, I get my sour cream ready. When I went to Mexico they piped the sour cream over dishes rather than in one big blob. So now that is what I do – it distributes the sour cream more evenly. Mix the sour cream and cream together in a bowl (this is known as Mexican cream) so it's thinner. Spoon the sour cream into a snaplock bag and snip off a small tip in the corner. When the cheese is melted, pipe over the sour cream in a fast zigzag motion. Top with guacamole. Garnish with black sesame seeds and coriander. Serve a lime cheek on the side.

GUACAMOLE

This is such an easy dip to make up – easily just as good with corn chips on it's own. Or I love it with roast chicken.

2 large avocados – I like Hass avocados
1 tablespoon sour cream
Juice of 1–2 limes

Makes 1 heaped cup
Time: Easy as

Scoop out the flesh of the avocados into a bowl, discarding the stone. Mash with a fork, then fold through the sour cream. This gives an extra creaminess to the guacamole. Add the lime juice and season well. Stir and taste. If you would like more lime, add extra.

Other variations: you can add chopped coriander, a small, finely diced red onion or some chilli. I like to keep mine plain so it's all about the avocado.

BEER BATTERED PRAWN TACOS WITH PINEAPPLE AND A CREAMY JALAPEÑO SAUCE

I love a good beer batter – one that is light and crisp. Use this recipe for fish or something like deep fried courgette flowers. These tacos have an interesting flavour – crunch, sweetness, heat – it has all that I need!

FOR THE BEER BATTER PRAWNS

1 egg white
¾ cup flour
½ teaspoon flaky sea salt
1 teaspoon castor sugar
220ml (7.7oz) beer, chilled (Pilsner, Pale Ale or you could use soda)
500g (1 lb 2oz) raw prawns
Canola or vegetable oil for frying

FOR THE JALAPENO DRESSING

½ cup natural thick yoghurt
½ cup mayonnaise
2 tablespoons lime juice
4 tablespoons jalapenos, less if you want less heat, of jalapeno (I used sliced jarred ones)
1 teaspoon honey

FOR THE PINEAPPLE SALSA

1 pineapple, small diced
2 tablespoons lime juice
½ small red onion, finely diced

TO SERVE

12–16 corn tortillas (I made blue corn tortillas see recipe page 84)
¼ red cabbage, finely sliced
Small bunch chives coriander

Serves 4–5 (3–4 tacos per person)
Time: Takes time

For the beer batter: Beat the egg white until they are stiff and set aside (this will make the batter really light). Combine the flour, salt and sugar together in a large bowl and whisk in the beer, little by little, about ⅔ to begin with. Then fold in the egg white. If you need to add more beer, add the rest. The batter should be thick. Chill in the fridge for 30 minutes.

For the jalapeno dressing: Combine all the ingredients together, I used a blender, but you could whisk by hand in a bowl or shake in a jar. Taste and season with salt and pepper. Set aside.

For the pineapple salsa: Combine all the ingredients together in a bowl. Taste and season with salt and pepper.

To serve: Have everything ready to serve – the dressing, pineapple, and tortillas, before you fry the prawns so that they are served hot. I always serve tacos DIY style – everyone makes their own, so lay everything out on the table.

Get a tray ready lined with a few paper towels. Set aside. Heat the oil in a large pot on a medium/high heat. You don't want the oil to come any further up than half way. Prawns float on the top of oil so they will need to be turned. I use a 'spider' tool for this (an Asian slotted wire spoon). Heat the oil to 190°C (375°F) – or I test it simply by putting the end of a wooden spoon into the oil. If bubbles from around the wooden stick, it's ready. Dip the prawns one at a time into the batter, tapping off excess on the side of the bowl, then carefully drop into oil. Working quickly, repeat and I cook in my large pot around 12 at a time. When golden brown (around 2–3 minutes) – remove and drain on the paper towels, season immeadiately with flaky sea salt. Repeat with remaining prawns until they are all fried.

To assemble, put some cabbage on the bottom followed by some pineapple. Top with some prawns, a little dressing and some chives. Eat immediately.

COURGETTE FLOWER AND HALLOUMI QUESADILLAS WITH ROASTED POBLANO AND TOMATILLO SALSA

When we were in Mexico we saw stands selling these courgette (and squash blossom) quesadillas and until that trip, I would never have thought to use them in this way. It is such a delicate courgette flavour and I love it with a punchy salsa on the side. If you don't grow courgettes or don't have access to the flowers, you can use grated courgette instead. Poblanos chillies are a mellow chilli so this is a good one for kids or chilli beginners (but I added a serrano chilli to mine, which are really hot). Tomatillos are known as Mexican husk tomatoes – they are green with a papery husk and have a tart taste. If you want to have a go at growing both of these yourself, see my "Pantry items" on page 192 for seed stockists. If you can't get a hold of poblanos or tomatillos – make a red salsa instead using the same amount of red tomatoes and a long red chilli instead. It will be a completely different flavour profile, but it will still be delicious! This salsa is so good with just some corn chips or as an accompaniment to tacos!

FOR THE SALSA

Makes: 2 cups

10 tomatillos – capes removed

2 poblano chilli

1 Serrano chilli (optional)

4 cloves garlic, skin on

1 onion, quartered

2 tablespoons olive oil

1 small bunch of coriander stalks (reserve leaves for enchilada garnish)

¼ cup water

1 teaspoon honey

1 tablespoon lime juice

FOR THE QUESADILLAS

2 tablespoons olive oil

1 onion, diced

2 cloves garlic, crushed

Zest 1 lemon

25 courgette flowers, stamen removed (or 2 cups grated courgette)

8 flour tortillas

200g (7oz) halloumi

2 cups grated mozzarella

Cooking spray

Lime wedges to serve

Serves: 4 as a snack

Time: Easy as

Preheat the grill to 200°C (390°F) on fan. Line a tray with foil.

Put the tomatillos, chilli, garlic and onion on the tray and rub with the olive oil. Grill for around 10 minutes until some of the ingredients are slightly blackened and charred. Pop the garlic out of the skins (leave on while roasting to protect the garlic from burning) and add to a food processor with the tomatillos, chilli, onion, water, honey and lime juice and blend until smooth. Taste and season with salt and pepper.

Heat a cast iron skillet on a medium/high heat. Once hot, add the oil and the onions with a pinch of salt and pepper and cook for around 4 minutes or until translucent. While they are cooking cut the courgette flowers into chunks, I cut mine into thirds. Add the garlic and lemon zest to the pan with the onions and cook for a further minute before adding the flowers. Cook until they just begin to wilt and then remove and set aside on a plate.

Clean the skillet out and return to a medium heat. Slice the halloumi into thin strips. Spray the pan with cooking spray and place one tortilla down, followed by some halloumi, ½ cup grated mozzarella an ¼ of the courgette flower mix making sure that the filling goes to the edges then place another tortilla on top. Spray the top with a little cooking spray and flip when the bottom side is browned. You don't want to cook on a high heat as it will brown before the cheese has melted. When both sides are brown, cut into quarters. Repeat until they are all made. Eat with a squeeze of lime (to cut through the cheese) and lots of salsa!

POSH FISH 'N' CHIPS

This is such an easy fuss-free weekday meal. The fish I used is already cooked, a wood smoked salmon – so all you need to do is make the dressing and wedges. If you're not a huge fan of salmon and would like to use a different fish, go ahead, the fish used in my fish tacos (page 87) would work well here also. My inspiration for this dish was to use salmon in a convenient way, with a dressing that uses all the flavours of a tartar sauce but with a twist. For the spiced potato wedges, I have seen chefs use curry powder in the batter for fish, so I decided to use that same flavour but on the wedges instead – and it worked so well. The wedges would also go really well with burgers!

FOR THE WEDGES
8 medium floury potatoes
½ cup flour
1 dry chicken stock cube
1 tablespoon hot curry powder
A pinch cayenne pepper – more if you want it hot
¼ cup olive oil

FOR THE SALMON
400g (14oz) fillet natural wood-smoked salmon
125g (4.7oz) bag watercress
Lemon wedges
Preserved lemon yoghurt dressing (see recipe below)

Serves: 4
Time: A little bit of effort

Preheat oven to 200°C (390°F) on fan bake. Line a large tray with baking paper and set aside.

Bring a large pot of water to the boil and season with salt once boiling. Meanwhile, scrub the potatoes well, (I use a wire brush) leaving the skins on. Cut into quarters and each quarter into half again to make wedge shapes. Once the water is boiling, put the wedges into the water, cover with a lid and boil for 5 minutes. While the potatoes are cooking, in a large bowl combine the flour, crumble over the chicken stock cube, the garlic powder, ½ teaspoon each of salt and pepper and mix well. After 5 minutes, drain the potatoes and then shake gently to fluff the potatoes up. By fluffing them you will rough up the edges and get nice crispy bits. Add to the mixing bowl with flour and spices and toss well to combine. Put the wedges on the prepared tray, discarding any leftover flour. Drizzle with olive oil and bake for 30 minutes or until golden and crunchy.

To serve: Watercress wilts really quickly, within minutes, so plate up just before serving. Arrange the watercress on a platter and flake the salmon over the top in chunks. Serve the preserved lemon dressing in a mug on the side. Serve with the spiced wedges and let everyone help themselves.

PRESERVED LEMON YOGHURT DRESSING

Preserved lemons are so easy to make (see my recipe page 146) but if you don't have them, then the zest from 1 lemon would work fine. This dressing goes so well with any fish and also makes a great dressing for potato salad!

½ cup yoghurt
½ cup mayonnaise
3 tablespoons gherkin juice or vinegar
2 teaspoons Dijon mustard
1 tablespoon capers, finely chopped
½ preserved lemon, yellow rind only, finely chopped
Small bunch parsley, finely chopped
½ teaspoon castor sugar
Olive oil to serve

Shake the yoghurt, mayonnaise, gherkin juice, mustard, capers, preserved lemon, parsley and castor sugar in a jar. Taste and season with salt and pepper. Pour into a jug or mug to serve in. Drizzle over a little olive oil and season with a little extra pepper.

Time: Easy as

CRISPY FISH WITH SPRING VEGETABLES, BABY POTATOES AND BASIL AIOLI

This is such a delicious fresh and seasonal dinner. I love the basil in the aioli as it gives it a pesto vibe and adds that extra something special. If you can't find fish with the skin on, it will still work just as well without. Use your favourite fish, a soft flaky white fish works best here.

BASIL AIOLI

4 free range egg yolks
2–3 tablespoons lemon or lime juice
1 tablespoon rice wine vinegar
2 teaspoons Dijon mustard
1 fat clove garlic, crushed
2 tightly packed cups basil leaves
1 ½ cups canola oil

FOR THE VEGETABLES

4 cups chicken stock
18 baby potatoes, halved (6 halves per person)
2 bunches asparagus, trimmed, cut on an angle into 3cm pieces
2 handfuls green beans, top end trimmed
1 bag snow peas
1 cup frozen peas

FOR THE FISH

6x 150g (5.5oz) fish fillets, skin on (soft, flaky white fish)
4 tablespoons olive oil
50g (1.7oz) butter

TO SERVE

1 medium fennel bulb, core cut out and very thinly sliced (I used my mandolin)
Fennel fronds
A handful baby basil leaves
Borage flower pods (optional)

Serves: 6
Time: A little bit of effort

For the basil aioli: In a food processor, mix up the egg yolks, 2 tablespoons lemon or lime juice, mustard, garlic, basil, a pinch of salt and pepper until the basil is finely chopped. While it's blending, slowly pour in the canola oil (don't pour too fast or the mayo won't get thick). Taste, season with more salt, pepper and a little extra lemon or lime juice if you need. Set aside.

For the vegetables: Bring the chicken stock to the boil. Add the potatoes and cook until almost tender. Add the beans and the asparagus and cook for 2 minutes. Then add the snow peas and peas and cook for a further 1 minute. Drain and set aside.

For the fish: Preheat oven to 50°C (120°F).

While the vegetables are cooking, heat a large cast iron skillet on a medium high heat with half the olive oil and butter. Season the skin with salt. Once the butter is melted and has begun to bubble, add the fish, 3 fillets at a time so not to over crowd the pan. Place in the pan skin side down. I hold the fish down with my hands so the fish doesn't curl up applying quite a bit of pressure. Hold there for about 30 seconds. Cook for approx. 2 minutes, until you can see the edges underneath start to go brown and the fish around the outside turns white. Flip and cook for a further 1 minute. Rest in the oven while you cook the rest of the fish with remaining oil and butter.

To serve: Divide the potatoes and vegetables between the plates. Add the fennel over the top. Place a piece of fish on top skin side up. Spoon over a generous blob of basil aioli, don't put over the top of the fish or it will make the crispy skin soggy. Scatter over the basil leaves, fennel fronds and borage pods if using. Finish with a little pepper and some flaky sea salt over the fish.

ROASTING WHOLE FISH

I have never been one to go for whole fish. The convenience of prepared fillets are just that, convenient. But as a single income family, one way to eat fish more regularly and affordably is to buy fish whole. It is much cheaper. I have to say that I am guilty of not knowing how to fillet fish, but I am learning and that will be something that I will keep practicing. The other good thing about filleting my own fish is that I can keep the skin on, which I also like. It is a little fiddly and we probably ate a lot slower being cautious of bones, but that's never a bad thing. I served this with a potato salad (see recipe page 136) and an asparagus and fennel coleslaw (See recipe page 128).

1.5kg (3.3lbs) whole fish of your choice,
    gutted and scaled (choose something
    fresh)*
2 lemons, sliced
4 bay leaves
1 large bulb fennel, slice (fronds used as
    garnish)
1 small bunch of soft herbs (I used
    tarragon, you could use dill or parsley)
75g (2.5oz) butter
A drizzle of olive oil

Serves: 4
Time: A little bit of effort

Preheat oven to 200°C (390°F).

Lightly score the fish in three places on both sides, almost to the bone but not all the way through. This will help the fish cook evenly. Fill the belly of the fish with half of the fillings. Arrange the rest of the ingredients on the top of the fish tying with kitchen string to hold. Drizzle with olive oil. Dot with butter and season with salt and pepper. Take a large sheet of tin foil and wrap the fish up creating a little bag so the steam doesn't escape.

Bake on a tray for around 40 minutes. You can test that the fish is cooked by removing the ingredients from the top and seeing if the flesh of the fish pulls away from the bone with ease. If it doesn't, wrap it back up put back in for another 3–4 minutes and check again.

Once cooked, I laid the fish out on a large platter on the table with the salads and everyone just helped themselves. You can use two forks and lift the fillets from the bone if you prefer. Be careful of the bones. Enjoy.

* Search online for sustainable fish to eat in your country.

CRAYFISH AND SAFFRON AIOLI

Whenever my husband and brother go for a dive, if the conditions are good, they usually always come home with crayfish. I always feel nervous about cooking this expensive product. I've made everything from salads to ravioli with crayfish, but I think my favourite way to eat it is simply cooked and chilled. If you want to get a bit fancy with it, then add a nice mayo on the side, like this saffron aioli to dip bits of the meat in to. When we ate this dish, we ate the tails with a green salad and potatoes first, and then the second course, sitting down to the delicious job of picking, cracking and eating the meat from the legs.

3–4 crayfish
Flaky sea salt

FOR THE SAFFRON AIOLI
1 good pinch saffron
4 egg yolks
2–3 tablespoons lemon juice
1 clove garlic, crushed
Salt and pepper
1 cup canola oil

TO SERVE
A few tarragon and dill leaves
Lemon wedges

Serves: 3–4
Time: Takes time for the crayfish
to chill

The first thing you need to do if you are dealing with live crayfish, is put them in the freezer for at least 30 minutes to euthanise them.

Bring two large pots of water to the boil then add 2 tablespoons of sea salt (or you can boil them in sea water). The time that you cook them for is dependent on their weight, I usually time 8 minutes per 600g. You can tell they are cooked when they are bright orange. Some people like theirs to be slightly translucent, but I like mine cooked till the flesh is white. If you cook them and then cut them open to realise that you haven't cooked them long enough, just heat a large frying pan or skillet on a medium high heat, rub the crays with a little butter and cook for about 1–1 ½ minutes longer (flesh side down). You know the crays are cooked well when the meat comes out of the shell with ease.

To cook: Place crayfish head first into the water making sure they are fully submerged. Cover with a lid and set your timer. While they are cooking, fill the sink with cold water and ice. When the crays are cooked, submerge into the ice water bath in the sink to stop them from cooking further. Chill in the fridge until you are ready to serve.

To make the aioli: In a small frying pan, over a medium/high heat, toast the saffron for a few minutes to release the flavour, tossing often. Remove and put into a small glass. Crumble the saffron with your fingers and top with a little hot water.

Put the eggs, 2 tablespoons lemon juice, garlic, salt and pepper and the saffron water into a blender and wiz on low. Slowly pour the oil in so that you have a thick and creamy aioli. Taste. Add more salt, pepper and lemon juice if it needs it.

To serve: Cut the crayfish in half with a sharp knife. Cut the tails from the bodies. Put on a serving plate, garnish with herbs, wedges of lemon and the aioli on the side.

INDIAN FISH CURRY

On cold grey days I love a warm comforting curry, and homemade spinach flatbreads or chapatis (both in my bread section, page 31) are the perfect thing to mop up all that sauce. This curry has got a good kick to it. If you don't like heat, leave out the green chillies and look for Kashmiri chilli powder instead as it's milder. This recipe would also be good with chicken too. I would go for thighs, cutting them into quarters. If you have an Indian spice store in your city it will be easy to source all of the ingredients in this recipe, and pretty cheap too! The spices tend to be much cheaper than supermarket brands as they buy them in bulk and package them themselves. If you haven't visited an Indian supermarket before, just search for one in your area online or if there are Indian people in your community, don't be shy, ask them if they can recommend a good supply store. The cool thing about food is that it can bring people together and forms a talking point.

FOR THE RICE
1 tablespoon ghee, melted
1 large mug basmati rice
2 large mugs boiling water

FOR THE CURRY
2 heaped tablespoons tamarind*
2 tablespoons ghee (or butter)
1 large onion, diced
1 thumb size piece ginger, peeled and grated
4 cloves garlic, crushed
30 fresh curry leaves
2 green chillies, whole
1 teaspoon black mustard seeds
1 teaspoon yellow mustard seeds
1 teaspoon fenugreek seeds
2 teaspoons hot garam masala
2 teaspoons hot chilli powder
2 teaspoons FairTrade unrefined sugar
1 teaspoon salt
2 teaspoons tomato paste
1x 400g (14oz) tin chopped tomatoes
1 cup coconut cream
750g (1.1lbs) fish (I used terakihi)
130g (4.6oz) green beans (I used Indian long beans, trimmed and cut in half)

TO SERVE
Chapatis (see recipe page 39)
Extra sliced green chilli (optional)

Serves: 4–5
Time: A little bit of effort

For the rice: Now my method is a little different, I use my Mum's technique which is in the microwave. If you want to do yours on a stove top or in a rice cooker, by all means, go ahead. Toss the rice and salt through the melted ghee in a microwave proof dish then pour over the boiling water and stir well. Cover, and microwave on high for 13 minutes. Remove and see if it's cooked (each microwave is different) if the liquid isn't quite absorbed, cook again for 2 minutes at a time. Fluff with a fork then cover again and let it sit for at least 5 minutes.

For the curry: Put the tamarind into a bowl and pour over 1 cup boiling water and set aside. The tamarind is going to give the sour element to the curry.

Heat the ghee in a cast iron skillet or large frying pan over a medium high heat. Add the onion and cook for 1–2 minutes, stirring until it goes slightly translucent but not browned. Add the ginger, garlic, curry leaves and green chillies (whole) and stir, frying for about 1 minute. Then add the seeds, spices, sugar and salt and stir, cooking for a further 1 minute. Add the tomato paste and tinned tomatoes – stir well then turn down the heat to a medium heat and simmer for 8–10 minutes, stirring occasionally.

While the sauce is simmering, take the soaked tamarind and push the liquid through a sieve. You don't want any of the solids or tamarind seeds, just the liquid and thick sieved bits that you can scrape from the bottom of the sieve. Discard the solids left in the sieve. Mix the sieved liquid up and add ¼ cup to the curry. Taste. If you want to add more to get the right balance for you, add a little more. It should have a good balance of heat, sweet (from the sugar) and sour.

Cut the fish into large 5cm (2 inch) chunks. Once the sauce has simmered, add the coconut cream, stir and bring back up to a simmer. Add the fish to the sauce, stir gently, cover and cook for 5 minutes. In the last 3 minutes of cooking, add the beans to the curry. Remove from the heat. Serve with rice and chapatis. Garnish with extra chillies if you want.

* If you can't source tamarind, you could use lemon juice instead, to taste.

LEMON AND HERB COUSCOUS SALAD

This is such a fresh salad with all the herbs and lemon through it – the perfect accompaniment to fish and especially the roasted salmon recipe below. It would also work well with chicken or as a side to take along to a BBQ. Feel free to switch up the herbs – I just used what I had in my garden, but any soft herbs would be nice. Also, when you go to buy Israeli couscous it is also sometimes known as 'pearl' couscous.

2 cups Israeli couscous
Zest 2 large lemons
Juice 1–2 lemons
¼ cup olive oil
¼ cup pine nuts, roasted
½ cup each of chopped mint, flat leaf
   parsley, coriander and chives

Serves: 4 as a side
Time: Easy as

Bring a large pot of salted water to a boil. Drop in your couscous and cook for 8 minutes or until al dente. As soon as it has cooked, drain and return to the pot (off the heat) and add the lemon zest, juice from 1 lemon, the olive oil and a good pinch of flaky salt and pepper and toss well to combine. At this stage the salad needs to completely cool before adding the herbs, otherwise the herbs will wilt and go black from the heat of the couscous. Once the couscous has cooled, reserve a handful of herbs to garnish, and fold the remaining herbs through the salad with the pine nuts. Taste and check for seasoning. See if you would like more lemon juice. If you are serving this salad with the roasted salmon, set aside while you prepare the fish to go with it.

ROASTED SALMON WITH A CRÈME FRAICHE DRESSING

By roasting salmon or any fish you can cook many portions at one time. It's delicious with dill and lemon crème fraiche as a dressing – dill and lemon with fish ... can't go wrong! Serve with some boiled new potatoes tossed in butter and herbs with some greens on the side – or with my lemon and herb couscous salad.

4 x 175g (6oz) fillets of salmon, pin boned
   (I cook with skin on to help hold it's
   shape)
 A little olive oil
Flaky sea salt

FOR THE CREME FRAICHE
½ cup creme fraiche juice
1 lemon
1 small bunch dill, chopped and extra
   to serve
lemon cheeks to serve

Serves: 4
Time: Easy as

Preheat oven to 200°C (390°F) and line a tray with baking paper and place salmon on the tray skin side down. Rub with a little bit of olive oil and season with flaky sea salt. Roast for around 8 minutes or until the salmon is cooked to your liking. To test – remove tray from the oven and take a small paring knife and gently cut into the thickest part of the salmon, it should be slightly translucent but not raw. Don't worry about any incision marks in the salmon; you can cover those up with a dollop of crème fraiche. If it's not cooked, return to the oven and cook at 1 minute intervals until it is cooked. When cooked, remove from oven and cover loosely with foil until you are ready to serve. Before serving and plating, I peel off the skin.

For the crème fraiche, mix all of the ingredients together in a bowl. Check for seasoning. Serve a large dollop on top of the salmon with extra dill and lemon on the side. Serve with the couscous salad (above).

PULLED PORK SLIDERS

Shoulder is my favourite cut of meat – it's cheap and when slow cooked it's soft, full of flavour and just pulls apart. This pork would also work well in a pulled pork taco. But in the brioche buns, it's the perfect weekend food! Use my brioche dough recipe to make 12 buns or buy some store-bought buns for an easier option.

FOR THE DRY RUB

4 tablespoons brown sugar

2 tablespoons onion powder

1 tablespoon mustard powder

2 tablespoons paprika

1 teaspoons fennel seeds

2 teaspoons black pepper

1 teaspoon cayenne pepper

2 tablespoons olive oil

2kg (4.5 lbs) free range pork shoulder, bone in

FOR THE WHISKY BBQ SAUCE

½ cup ketchup

¼ cup rice wine vintage

3 tablespoons brown sugar

2 cloves garlic, crushed

A pinch of cayenne pepper

2–3 tablespoons whisky

FOR THE SLAW

¼ cup sunflower seeds

¼ red cabbage

½ white cabbage

1 green apple

1 tablespoon lime juice

¼ cup currants

1 teaspoon celery seeds

FOR THE DRESSING

3 tablespoons mayonnaise

1 tablespoon milk

2 tablespoons gherkin juice (from a jar of pickles)

1 teaspoon Dijon mustard

½ teaspoon castor sugar

12 brioche buns to serve

Serves: 4–5

Time: Takes time / marinate overnight

Combine all of the dry rub ingredients together in a bowl and mix well. Drizzle the pork with the olive oil and rub the pork well with the dry rub mix. Put into a small roasting dish and cover with plastic wrap. Marinate overnight in the fridge.

Next day, preheat oven to 160°C (320°F). Put ½ cup water into the bottom of the dish with the pork. Cover with tin foil and bake, covered for 3 hours. Remove foil and cook for a further 2 ½ hours until the pork pulls apart with ease with two forks. Glaze the cooked pork with pan juices and let it rest, covered loosely with foil while you prepare the accompaniments.

For the BBQ sauce: Combine all of the ingredients together in a small pot, whisking well to combine (add whisky to taste). Cook over a medium/high heat until it thickens slightly and gets glossy.

For the slaw: Toast the seeds over a medium/high heat until browned. Set aside to cool. Slice the cabbages as finely as you can and add to a bowl. Then slice apple into matchsticks and toss them with lime juice to give them a nice sour taste and stop them from browning. Add to the bowl with the cabbage and the currants, sunflower seeds and celery seeds. Shake all the dressing ingredients together in a jar. Add half of the dressing to the slaw. Toss well, taste and season to your liking with salt and pepper. Serve the extra dressing on the side.

To serve: Pull the pork with two forks so that it shreds. Take a bun and split it. Spread top and bottom with BBQ sauce. Add a handful of slaw and top with pulled pork and a little extra BBQ sauce. Dig in!

MAC 'N' CHEESE

It is a tradition in our house, when my son has friends staying for a sleep over – this is the requested dinner. Kids love it and I love to serve it with a DIY salad on the side. I like mac 'n' cheese to be just that, macaroni and lots of cheese, but let me tell you, if you are hot sauce fiends like my husband and I are, hot sauce and mac 'n' cheese will change your life, it's the best combination ever! If you wanted to make this a little more inexpensive, just use a tasty melting cheese. I sometimes make it with just one cheese and it's still great! The parmesan gives it a real cheesy flavour and the mozzarella the stringiness!

500g (1 lb) macaroni
100g (3.5 oz) butter
¾ cup flour
1 bay leaf
3 cups milk
2 teaspoons Dijon mustard
Pinch nutmeg
2 cups grated Colby or Tasty cheese
½ cup grated parmesan
1 cup grated mozzarella
¾ cup reserved pasta water

TO TOP

½ cup panko breadcrumbs
1 cup grated Colby or Tasty cheese
2 tablespoons butter

Serves: 6
Time: A little bit of effort

Preheat oven to 180°C (350°F) fan grill.

Bring a large pot of water to the boil then salt. Add the macaroni and cook for 8 minutes. Reserve a cup of pasta water, drain the pasta. Set aside.

Meanwhile, melt the butter in a large pot over a medium/high heat. Once melted add the flour and cook for 1 minute, stirring continuously. Season with salt and pepper and the bay leaf, stir, then add 1 cup of the milk – mix with a whisk to get rid of the lumps (also using a wooden spoon to get out the clumps from the edge of the pot). Then add the remaining milk with the mustard and the nutmeg and give it a good whisk to combine. Turn off the heat and add the cheeses, stirring well. It will be thick once the cheese has melted. Use ½ – ¾ cup of the reserved pasta water to loosen the sauce. You want the sauce to be a runny yoghurt consistency – it thickens again when it bakes. Add the cooked macaroni and combine well with a wooden spoon.

Put into an oven proof dish and top with the cheese, then the breadcrumbs. Dot over the butter and put under the preheated grill for 8–10 minutes or until golden. The pasta is already cooked so it's just a matter of getting it browned and crunchy. Let it sit for a few minutes before serving with a salad.

DIY SALAD

A DIY salad is where I put all the ingredients of a salad into a bowl or on a platter with a dressing on the side and everyone makes their own – they grab the stuff they like and the amount of dressing they want.

½ cup sliced almonds
8 medium tomatoes, quartered
2 cups fresh mung bean sprouts
2 avocados, sliced
½ telegraph cucumber, deseeded and
  sliced
1 large bag of rocket
Microgreens (I used sorrel)
Salad dressing (see recipe page 140)

Serves: 6 as a side   Time: Easy as

Toast the almonds in a small frying pan over a medium high heat, tossing regularly until slightly brown and toasted. Remove and cool on a plate.

Arrange the rest of the DIY salad ingredients in sections so it's easy to grab. Add the almonds in a little bowl and serve the dressing on the side.

Note: you can use pumpkin seeds or sunflower seeds in place of the almonds and cos lettuce, baby spinach or Mesculin leaves instead of Rocket. Microgreens are optional.

BEEF BOURGUIGNON

This is my version of the classic French stew (Burgundy beef, because of the red wine). So comforting on a cold evening, and the trump card is the addition of horseradish to the mash. Horseradish and beef, this combination is a classic for a reason, it just works! I usually make double what I need and the next night I use the leftover stew as a filling in pasties or meat pies (see my recipe for Hand Pies on page 114)

2 tablespoons olive oil
1kg (2.2lbs) stewing steak
10 baby onions, peeled
4 carrots, peeled and sliced
4 cloves garlic, crushed
2 teaspoons FairTrade unrefined sugar
1 bottle Pinot Noir
3 tablespoons tomato paste
2 cups beef stock, hot
1 small bunch of rosemary and thyme
1 tablespoon butter
24 (350g/12oz) small button mushrooms,
    cut any larger ones in half

TO ADD AT THE END
1 tablespoon flour
1 tablespoon butter
A little parsley and some thyme leaves to
    garnish

Serves: 5 people
Time: Takes time

Preheat oven to 150°C (300°F).

Trim any excess fat off the steak and cut into a chunky dice, season the beef generously with salt and pepper. Heat 1 tablespoon of oil at a time in a large cast iron skillet over a high heat. Sear the beef in two batches, removing and adding to a medium sized roasting dish when done. Turn the heat down to medium and add the onions and the carrots and a small pinch of salt, cook for around 7 minutes until they start to soften. Add the garlic and cook for a further 30 seconds, then add the sugar and tomato paste, give it a good stir before pouring in the wine. Increase the heat to high, bring to the boil and cook for about 5 minutes. Pour this mix over the beef in the roasting dish, then top up with the hot beef stock. Tie the rosemary and thyme with kitchen string and place on top. Cover with foil and cook for 1 ½ hours.

Meanwhile, cook the mushrooms with the butter over a medium/high heat until brown, around 10 minutes. Set aside on a plate. Mix together on a board with a fork the flour and butter, setting aside for now. This is going to thicken the stew. At this stage I make the horseradish mash, which can be warmed later when serving. After 1 ½ hours, remove the stew from the oven and take foil off, discard rosemary and thyme stalks. Place the roasting dish on the stove top over a medium/high heat. Add the mushrooms, flour, and butter mixture and stir well. Let it bubble away and thicken for around 20 minutes. Taste and check seasoning, adjust if needed. Fill bowls or plates with mash. Top with stew and garnish with herbs.

HORSERADISH MASH

I tried all different mash combinations and flavours to go with this stew, and this was by far the best. Winner!

2kg (4.4lbs) medium floury potatoes
100g butter, room temperature
1 cup milk
1 cup cream
6 tablespoons horseradish cream

Serves: 5
Time: A little bit of effort

I used horseradish cream, which is more mild than fresh horseradish. If you are using fresh horseradish, use less and to taste. Peel and cut potatoes into quarters. Put them into a large pot and cover with water and season with salt. Cover pot and bring to the boil, cook until a knife goes through the centre of the potatoes with ease. In a medium sized pot, heat the milk, cream and horseradish cream together until hot but not boiling, then set aside. When the potatoes are cooked, drain well add the butter and mash. Put the mash through a potato ricer to get it super smooth, if you don't have one, a hand masher is fine. Add the liquid bit by bit until you get the consistency you like. Taste and season to taste.

HAND PIES WITH A FLAKY SHORTCRUST PASTRY

I only make these when I have leftovers to use as a filling. Leftover stew, curry, even beef and bean nacho mix. You don't need a lot to make it stretch out to make another meal. I use 1½ heaped tablespoons of filling in each hand pie. If you don't have quite enough leftovers, I usually bulk it out with some extra vegetables or a can of chickpeas. Two other fast options are making one large pie or using store-bought shortcrust pastry. Sometimes I feel like the idea is inspiration enough, and these hand pies are such a good way of turning leftovers into something new the next night.

250g (8.8oz) butter
1 cup hot water
2 ½ cups plain flour
1 cup wholemeal flour
1 level teaspoon salt

TO FILL
Approx. 2–3 cups of leftovers to use as a
    filling (or see my recipe for stew on page
    113)
1 small free range egg, beaten

NOTE: filling has to be completely cold
    before using so that the pastry doesn't
    go soggy or cook from the inside out.

TO SERVE
Rosemary
Relish and a green salad

Serves: Makes 10
Time: Takes time

Cut the butter into cubes and add to a small pot with the water. Over a high heat bring to a rapid boil ensuring that the butter has melted.

While that is coming up to heat, combine the flours and salt together in a bowl and make a well in the centre. Pour the butter and water mix into the well and mix to combine. Wrap the dough in plastic wrap and put in the fridge for 30 minutes.

Preheat oven to 180°C (350°F) and line a tray with baking paper.

After 30 minutes take the pastry out and divide into two so it's easy to roll. I used a breakfast bowl that is a 15cm (6in) circle as my cutter. Roll the pastry out on a lightly floured surface (cutting and making one at a time) to ½cm (¼in) thick. Put 1 ½ heaped tablespoons filling in the centre. Now, the 'hand' part of the pie, pick the pastry up and seal together to form a crescent shape. Holding the pie in your hand – place your finger under the edge of the pie to support the pasty and use a fork to press against the edge to form an indentation and further sealing. Place on a baking tray and repeat the process until finished.

Brush the pies with egg wash and bake for around 35–40 minutes or until golden and cooked through. Serve with relish, and a green or chop salad (see page 123).

GREEK STYLE CHICKEN WRAPS

This is the kind of eating that I love. Almost like a street food style dish at home. One of the best things I ate when I was in New York were these amazing chicken wraps. We stayed right in the city in Times Square, so there were all kinds of food carts dotted on every corner. The one we visited had a huge queue of people lining up at it (the first sign that you are at a good spot). For my version of chicken wraps, I begin by marinating the chicken overnight it will intensify the flavours incredibly. I have used all the flavours of Greece and it's banging with flavour. Try with my 'Spinach Flatbread' (recipe on page 40) or just grab some store-bought flatbreads if you want something more convenient. For a vegetarian option, replace chicken with long slices of eggplant (I wouldn't marinade these overnight – just 15 minutes would be fine).

1kg (2.2 lbs) boneless skinless free range chicken thighs
1 preserved lemon – skin only, pith removed, chopped (or zest of 1 lemon)
2 tablespoons olive oil
2 tablespoons dried Greek oregano* (or regular dried oregano)
4 cloves garlic, crushed
2 tablespoons honey

PRESERVED LEMON TZATZIKI
1 cup plain thick Greek yoghurt
½ preserved lemon (or zest 1 lemon)
1 long red chilli, deseeded
⅓ cucumber, deseeded, grated
1 small clove garlic
Small bunch mint, chopped
2 tablespoons olive oil and extra to cook

TO SERVE
8 wraps or flatbreads
1 bag of rocket
Big bunch flat leaf parsley
1 small red onion, sliced thinly*
1 red chilli
⅔ cucumber, deseeded thinly sliced
100g (3.5oz) feta, crumbled
Olive oil to drizzle

Makes 8 wraps
Time: Begin the day before for the marinating if possible / A little bit of effort

Ingredient notes before we begin:

* Greek oregano I bought from a speciality food store and it comes on the stick in long packs. Regular dried oregano is fine if you don't have the Greek variety.
* Soak the sliced onions in a bowl of water to take away that harsh onion taste. Drain before using.

For the chicken: Combine the chicken in a bag or bowl with the lemon, olive oil, oregano, garlic and honey. Season with a little salt and pepper and combine well. Set aside while you prepare your tzatziki or marinade overnight for best results.

For the tzatziki: Mix all of the ingredients together in a bowl. Check for seasoning.

To serve: Heat a cast iron skillet or large frying pan on a high heat. Cook the chicken in batches for around 2–3 minutes on each side or until cooked through. You want to try and get a nice crispy sear on the chicken. The honey in the marinade will help achieve it. Once all cooked, let the chicken rest for a few minutes before carving on an angle into slices.

I put all the fillings into bowls on the table and let everyone make their own. For mine, I spread a little tzatziki on the wraps in the centre. Top with some rocket, parsley, cucumber, red oinion. Add some chicken, a little more tzatziki, feta, chilli and some pepper (it won't need salt as the feta is salty) and drizzle with a little olive oil. Fold the bottom up first and then the two sides in. Wrap in a little lunch paper if you want.

SOUTHERN STYLE FRIED CHICKEN

Making your own fried chicken is great because you can use free range, you know it's fresh and you get to make it how you like it. I coat mine only once in the seasoned flour as I like a thin crispy coating. If you're the sort of person that likes lots of crunch, then make double the coating and double dip it for a thicker crust. Serve with potato salad and coleslaw for a real Southern style dinner.

2kg (4.4lb) free range chicken pieces – I used drumsticks and wings as they take less time to cook than thighs
2 cups buttermilk (or 2 cups milk with 2 tablespoons lemon juice)
2 litres canola oil for frying

DRY COATING
2 cups flour
2 tablespoons garlic powder
2 tablespoons onion powder
1 teaspoon smoked paprika
1 teaspoon mustard powder
2 teaspoons salt
2 teaspoons black pepper
½ teaspoon cayenne pepper (optional)

TO SERVE
Rosemary sprigs

Serves 6 with side salads
Time: Begin the day before (marinating) / Takes time

Note: If you want an extra kick to your fried chicken, add 2 tablespoons of your favourite hot sauce in with the buttermilk. Also, I coat the chicken in buttermilk and leave overnight in the fridge. I find that by doing that, the chicken is super juicy and soft. If you don't have time to do this, just dredge in buttermilk and dip into flour. In a bowl coat the chicken in buttermilk. Cover and refrigerate overnight or until you are ready to cook.

Heat the oil in a large heavy bottom pot to 180°C (350°F); I kept it on a medium heat. If the oil is too hot it will cook too quickly and the chicken will brown on the outside and be raw on the inside. Also, do not over fill the pot with oil – no more than half way up otherwise it could bubble over when cooking. While the oil is coming up to heat, combine all of the dry coating ingredients together in a bowl. Dip the buttermilk chicken pieces into the seasoned flour and set aside ready for frying. Line a tray with paper towels for draining and set to the side. Get some flaky salt and pepper close by. When the oil is hot carefully place the chicken in oil (I cook 6 pieces at a time), I use my metal slotted spoon to lower each piece in. Fry for 10–12 minutes, thighs take around 14–16 minutes. I set a timer so that I know it is neither overcooked nor undercooked. When cooked remove with a slotted spoon and place onto paper towels to absorb excess oil. Immediately season with salt and pepper when hot so that it sticks. You can test a piece by cutting into it close to the bone. The juices should run clear. Cover with foil (you can keep warm in a low oven if you wish) and repeat the process until all the chicken is cooked. Garnish with rosemary and serve with side salads.

Sides

This section is about picking and choosing a few salads or side dishes and putting a meal together. You might have some leftover Christmas ham and want to have a few salads to go with it for a meal, you might cook up a roast chicken and want some side dishes to serve alongside, or you can take salads in this section to work for lunch or to the next BBQ you are invited to.

My Mum is known for her salad repertoire, and we love when she invites us over, especially in summer. She has cold meats and a huge selection of salads and sides to go with them, all in the middle of the table and we all just help ourselves. This love for putting salads together I have definitely inherited. Also in this section is her stuffing roll recipe which we all think is her signature dish! It would make an excellent side dish to any roast dinner. We only get to eat it once a year at Christmas but we crave it year round, come November everyone is talking about it! Now that I have the recipe I am tempted to make it more often, but I'm scared that if I do we all won't look forward to the tradition of it only once a year. I love how food can be so directly linked to a time and person so much – that is what makes certain dishes so special.

This section is so versatile and adaptable and I have given suggestions for when you can switch things around and make it your own.

COURGETTE SALAD

In the warmer months one of my favourite things to grow in our garden are courgettes, mostly for their flowers which you can stuff with ricotta and herbs like they do in Italy or in Mexico, they use them in quesadillas with cheese. From just two plants, you will have a never ending supply of courgettes over summer and will have to think of ways to use them up. This is one of my creations. You can bulk the salad out with baby spinach and some cooked quinoa if you like.

4 courgette, 2 yellow and 2 green
Small bunch mint
100g (3.5oz) feta
¼ cup pine nuts, roasted
Dry chilli flakes or fresh chilli (finely diced)
A little olive oil
Juice of 1 lemon

Time: Easy as
Serves: 4 as a side

Take a speed peeler and peel long ribbons of the courgette. When you get to the seeds, flip and peel the other side. I don't use the seedy middle part (save that for a stir fry or something). Add to a mixing bowl. Take the bigger leaves of mint and rip apart with your fingers and reserve any little leaves for garnish. Crumble over most of the feta, reserving some for garnish. Toss through most of the pine nuts saving some for garnish also. Mix together in the bowl with some chilli flakes, a little olive oil and lemon juice to taste. You don't want to add too much or it will go soggy, just enough to loosen and flavour. Taste and see if you want to add more lemon, chilli or pepper. You might not need salt as the feta is salty. Put onto a serving plate or bowl – top with reserved mint, feta and pine nuts. Add a little extra chilli if you like and some pepper. Drizzle with a tiny bit more oil and serve immediately.

CHOP SALAD

I make this salad whenever we have takeaways. I'm the only cook in my house, so when I don't feel like cooking (which isn't that often) this is the salad that I make to go with fish and chips or pizza. I have to have a salad with food like that so I don't feel "UGH" after. The salad has to be fast to make, to be able to put it together before my hubby returns from the chippy. I call it my chop salad, because I quickly chop everything and throw it together. For a fast grab-and-go, I always have pre-roasted seeds in containers in my cupboards. To do this, just roast a big batch of seeds in a 180°C (350°F) oven on a tray, single layer, for around 7 minutes or until brown and toasted. Keeps for months in an air tight container.

10 small tomatoes
4 radish (French breakfast)
½ cucumber
1 handful roasted sunflower seeds
½ red capsicum
1 large handful of fresh mung beans
  sprouts
1 tablespoon sesame seeds (or pumpkin)
Herbs – two of these: mint, flat leaf
  parsley, chives, tarragon, coriander, dill
A drizzle of olive oil
A squeeze of lemon juice (or a little
  vinegar)

Serves: 4 as a side
Time: Easy as

Note: other optional ingredients you can use are: avocado, red onion or spring onion, apple, currants or raisins, grated carrot, feta.

Halve or quarter tomatoes and add to a mixing bowl. Thinly slice the radish, I used a mandolin, add to the bowl. Cut the cucumber in half lengthwise, deseed scraping out the seeds with a teaspoon and slice. Dice the capsicum and add to the mixing bowl with the cucumber, mung beans, seeds and herbs. Dress with olive oil and a little lemon and some salt and pepper. Taste and adjust seasoning if needed.

CHILLI JAM

Chilli jam is such a versatile condiment. Use it to marinade meats like chicken or beef before adding them to the BBQ or putting under the grill, to glaze and baste meats while they are cooking to keep adding layers of flavour. Add a spoonful of it to a stew to give it a flavour boost, eat it with sour cream with potato wedges, or simply with cheese on crackers. I also love to add a tablespoon of it to my simple salad dressing recipe and use it to dress Asian style salads.

8 red chillies (I used 6 long red chillies
    and 2 red jalapeños)
1 red capsicum
2 red onions
1 thumb size piece of ginger
2 double kaffir lime leaves
1 bulb garlic (around 10 cloves)
2 tablespoons canola oil
3 tablespoons FairTrade unrefined sugar
2–3 tablespoons lime juice
1–2 tablespoons fish sauce
1 tablespoon soy sauce

Sterilise jars and lids. Roughly chop chillies and add to a food processor. Discard seeds and stem from capsicum, roughly chop and add to the processor with the onions and ginger – both also roughly chopped. Cut and discard centre vein from lime leaves and slice, add to the processor also. Peel cloves of garlic and add to the processor and blend until smooth. Heat the oil over a medium high heat in a large skillet or frying pan. Add the chilli paste and cook for around 3–4 minutes, stirring continuously until it smells fragrant and begins to thicken slightly. Add the sugar and cook with the paste for a further 1 minute. Add 2 tablespoons lime juice, 1 tablespoon of fish sauce and soy sauce and mix well. Taste and if you need further acidity or saltiness add a little more lime or fish sauce. Spoon into sterilised jars. Keeps well in the fridge for several months.

Makes: 2 small jars   Time: Easy as

HEIRLOOM TOMATO SALAD

This salad is the taste of summer! One of the things that I dream about during winter are the tomatoes I will grow in the warmer months. There are so many different varieties of tomatoes available in all different colours, shapes and sizes. I love the addition of sundried tomatoes here in the salad, it gives another dimension of tomato flavour. I also love chilli with tomato and my chilli jam goes so well with this salad. Seasonal ingredients taste so good together – tomatoes, basil, chilli – yum! Serve as it is to a side with grilled fish or BBQ meats or serve as a starter and top toasted ciabatta bread to make bruschetta. Basil aioli (see recipe page 96) would also be such a delicious alternative here in place of the chilli jam.

1 small red onion
10 heirloom tomatoes of your choice
6–8 sundried tomatoes
5 teaspoons chilli jam (or you could use
    1 long red chilli, diced)
About 3 tablespoons oil from the sundried
    tomato jar
15 baby basil leaves
Juice of 1 medium lemon

Cut the red onion in half and then into thin slices. Put into a bowl of water – by soaking the onion in water, it takes some of the harsh raw taste away and mellows it. Set onion aside while you prepare the rest of the salad. Slice the tomatoes up – I like to slice them depending on the shape. Cutting long slices, circles, wedges, some thick and chunky and some thin. Arrange them on a platter or in a bowl. Cut the sundried tomatoes in half, leaving smaller ones whole and place around the salad. Spoon dollops of chilli jam around the salad. Drizzle over the sundried tomato oil and squeeze over some lemon juice. Garnish with basil leaves. Season with salt and pepper.

Serves: 4 as a side (depending on size of the tomatoes)   Time: Easy as

124

BEETROOT, GOAT CHEESE AND WALNUT SALAD WITH A PINK YOGHURT DRESSING

Beetroot and goat cheese is a classic combination because of the deep and earthy flavour of the beetroot, especially when roasted, and the sharpness and slight sourness of the goat cheese. These opposite flavours therefore are a good balance. I grow Chioggia beetroots in my garden, the stripy ones, and I like to serve these raw in the salads because once they are cooked, they lose their stripes and vibrancy. If you don't have them, just leave them off and use only the roasted beetroots. This salad would make a pretty starter for a dinner party and the yoghurt/beetroot dressing also goes really well with salmon and new baby potatoes.

8 small red beetroot
4 cloves garlic, whole, skins left on
2 tablespoons oil
1 cup walnut halves
2 tablespoons honey

FOR THE DRESSING
2 of the red beetroot from above, once
   roasted
Garlic from above, once roasted
¼ cup Greek yoghurt
2 tablespoons lemon juice
2 tablespoons olive oil
1 teaspoon Dijon mustard
1 tablespoon honey
approx. ¼ cup milk

TO SERVE
2 Chioggia beetroot
Small bunch flat leaf parsley
Small handful dill
50g (1.7oz) goat cheese
Olive oil
juice 1 lemon
Beetroot Bulls blood micro greens
   (optional)

Serves: 6 as a starter
Time: Takes time

Preheat oven to 200°C fan bake (400°F).

Take a large sheet of tin foil and place on a baking tray. Put the 8 red beetroots in the centre with the garlic. Drizzle over the oil and season with salt and pepper. Wrap the foil up so it is a little parcel that the steam can't escape from. Roast for 40–50 minutes or until the beetroot is cooked. Insert a sharp knife into the centre to check the beets are cooked. If it goes in with ease, its ready. Set aside until cool enough to handle. Reserve and set aside 2 of the beetroots for the dressing as well as the garlic. When it is cool (wearing gloves if you don't want pink stained hands) peel the beetroots skin off but just rubbing with your hands, or cutting off with a paring knife. Cut each beet into quarters and each quarter in half again to get bite size wedges. Set aside.

Reduce oven to 180°C (350°F) and turn the fan off and switch to regular bake. Take a tray and line with baking paper. Spread walnuts on and drizzle with honey. Bake for 5 minutes, then remove from oven, give the walnuts a toss through the caramelised honey and return to the oven for around 3 minutes or until they are golden brown. Remove and cool.

For the dressing, squeeze the garlic out of the skins and add to a blender with the reserved beetroot, yoghurt, lemon juice, olive oil, mustard, honey and a good seasoning of salt and pepper. Blend until smooth, then slowly add enough milk so that you have the consistency you want. I kept mine reasonably thick so it didn't run all over the plate. Taste. If it needs a little more salt, pepper or lemon juice – add it.

To serve, with a mandolin (or awesome knife skills) slice the Chioggia beets as thin as you can. Divide roasted beets among plates, then rest the sliced Chioggia on roasted beetroot wedges. Add the herbs over top, I don't chop those, I like to see the shape of the leaves. Spoon over some of the dressing in the gaps then add the goat cheese in spots around the beetroot too. Drizzle over a little olive oil and a squeeze of lemon. Season with flaky sea salt and pepper. Finish with the micro greens.

GREEN BEANS WITH ALMONDS

The simplicity of just a few ingredients where they all complement each other is such a good thing. I love how easy this is to make and I serve these beans with things like meatloaf or roast meats.

500g green beans
¼ cup sliced almonds, toasted
Flaky sea salt
Good olive oil

Serves: 6 as a side
Time: Easy as

Bring a pot of water to the boil, big enough and with enough water to completely cover beans. Salt generously. While the water is coming up to the boil, trim the ends but leaving the pointy bit on the bean. Once the water is at a rolling boil, drop the beans in and set a timer for exactly 2 minutes. Drain and arrange on a small platter. Drizzle with oil, scatter over almonds and finish with some flaky salt. Serve immediately so they retain their colour and crunch. If not serving immediately, you can serve cold. Plunge the hot beans into ice water to 'shock' them after cooking to retain their bright green colour and crunch – drain well before serving.

ASPARAGUS AND FENNEL SLAW

By shaving thin ribbons of asparagus with a speed peeler you can eat this vegetable raw, which, we don't often do. I use a mandolin to cut the fennel – it's such a handy tool to have in the kitchen and is so fast I can never cut vegetables as paper thin with a knife and as quickly compared to using a mandolin. I really like how crunchy and healthy this raw slaw is, it really makes the vegetables shine. It's perfect to serve with pork or fish dishes as fennel goes so well with these two proteins.

2 bunches of asparagus
2 large carrots
2 large fennel, fronds reserved
1 small bunch of mint and flat leaf parsley,
  chopped
1 long red chilli
Chive flowers to garnish (optional)
Olive oil

DRESSING
¼ cup good olive oil
1 tablespoon lemon juice
1 tablespoon vinegar
1 heaped teaspoon Dijon mustard
1 level teaspoon runny honey (or castor
  sugar)

Serves 6 as a side
Time: Easy as

Wash and snap the asparagus ends then peel with a speed peeler to get long thin ribbons. Peel the carrots in the same way, then stack the ribbons on top of each other, cut the stack in half, then cut into fine match sticks. Cut the tough core out of the fennel then slice as thinly as you can. Set all of these aside in a large bowl. Deseed the chilli (you don't want an overpowering heat in this delicate salad, just a nice warm background heat) and cut in half lengthwise, then slice very finely. Add to the bowl with the cut vegetables. Toss together with the herbs.

Shake all of the dressing ingredients together in a jar with a good pinch of salt and pepper. Taste and check for seasoning. Pour over the slaw and gently toss with hands to combine, then serve in a clean bowl or platter. Garnish with reserved fennel fronds, chive flowers, a little extra black pepper and finish with a drizzle of olive oil.

BROCCOLI SALAD WITH A FRESH CHILLI AND HERB MAYONNAISE DRESSING

A great salad to take to work, or I like it as a side dish to roast chicken. I love its crunchiness and the punchy dressing that goes with it.

2 large broccoli heads
½ cup sliced almonds
1 tablespoon canola oil
1 large red onion, halved and sliced thinly
4 slices free range streaky bacon

FOR THE CHILLI MAYO

1 long red chilli, finely diced
1 small bunch of herbs, finely chopped (I
    used chives, oregano and fennel fronds)
4 tablespoons mayonnaise
3 tablespoons lemon juice
2 tablespoons olive oil
1 tablespoon milk
1 teaspoon wholegrain mustard
Pinch FairTrade unrefined sugar

Serves: 3–4 as a side
Time: A little bit of effort

Bring a large pot of water to the boil. Cut broccoli florets into bite size pieces. When water is boiling, salt and add the broccoli and cook for exactly 2 minutes. While it's cooking get a large bowl of cold water with some ice cubes in it. Immediately scoop and plunge the cooked broccoli into the ice water to retain colour and crunch. Once cold, drain in a colander giving it a good shake and then place onto a clean tea towel to absorb excess water. You want to remove as much water as possible so it doesn't dilute the dressing.

In a skillet or frying pan over a medium/high heat, toast almonds for a few minutes until brown. Remove and set aside. Add the canola oil to the pan and cook the onion with a pinch of salt, stirring regularly so that it goes translucent but not browned. Remove from pan and set aside. Add the bacon and cook until crispy on both sides. Cool slightly then slice into strips. Add the broccoli to a bowl with the almonds, onions and bacon.

For the dressing: Set aside a little of the chilli and some of the herbs for garnish, then shake the remaining chilli and herbs in a jar with the rest of the dressing ingredients (it shouldn't need salt as the bacon is quite salty and salt has already been added to the broccoli and onions). Pour two thirds of the dressing over the broccoli in the bowl. Toss well and put into a clean bowl to serve. Dollop over remaining dressing and ganish with the remaining chilli and herbs. Drizzle over a little extra olive oil and some pepper.

FARRO SALAD WITH GRILLED EGGPLANT, FRESH PEAS, PINE NUTS AND PARMESAN

Farro is a grain that when cooked has a chewy texture and has a nutty taste which makes the perfect salad base. If you can't get a hold of it a good alternative is brown rice or pearl barley. I love the charred flavour of the eggplant, the freshness from the peas, the saltiness from the parmesan and the crunch of the pine nuts – so good! This salad would go really well with lamb and a little hummus on the side.

1 cup organic farro
2 cups water
1 bay leaf

FOR THE DRESSING

¼ cup olive oil
2 tablespoons chardonnay vinegar (or vinegar of your choice)
2 teaspoons wholegrain mustard
1 clove garlic, crushed finely
1 teaspoon honey

FOR THE REST OF THE SALAD

2 small eggplants
¼ cup olive oil
a large handful fresh peas (or frozen is fine)
3 tablespoons pine nuts, roasted
Zest of 1 lemon
Small bunch dill, (and/or mint or flat leaf parsley) chopped
30g (1oz) parmesan, you don't need much
A little olive oil to finish

Serves: 5–6 as a side
Time: Takes time

To cook the farro: Put the farro, water and a bay leaf in a pot with a good pinch of flaky sea salt and bring to the boil. Once boiling, reduce heat to medium/low and cook simmering with the lid on for about 25–30 minutes or until the majority of the water has evaporated. Fluff with a fork, cover again and let it sit, off the heat for 10 minutes.

For the dressing: Shake all of the dressing ingredients, the olive oil, vinegar, mustard, garlic, honey and salt and pepper together in a jar. Taste and see if it needs any extra seasoning or vinegar. Pour the dressing over the hot farro stirring well to combine and set aside until you are ready to use.

To grill the eggplant I actually use my Panini press (toasted sandwich maker). It has the bar marks on the top and it also cooks both sides at the same time so it's really fast. If you don't have one just cook in a griddle pan to get the lines or just a frying pan is fine too. Cut the stem off the eggplant at the top and slice into thin 1 cm (½ inch) thick slices. Brush each slice both sides with olive oil and season with salt and pepper. Grill in batches until all the eggplant has been cooked.

For the peas: Bring a pot of water to the boil. Drop the peas in (in their pods) and cook for exactly 1 ½ minutes. While they are cooking, get a large bowl with cold water and a few ice cubes in it ready. Plunge the cooked peas into the cold water to stop cooking and to retain the bright green colour. I popped some of the peas out of the pod and others I wanted to leave in the pod. I took a paring knife and cut into the seam of the pod slightly and carefully so it wouldn't disturb the peas then carefully peeled off one half of the pod. Totally not necessary, I only do it for presentation sake.

To plate: I wanted to serve on a board, but my board didn't have sides, so I took a piece of baking paper, screwed it up into a ball then opened it up and used this to put the salad on top, it held everything on the board nicely. Put the dressed farro on first. Ribbon over the eggplant giving it a little height if possible. Scatter over the peas and place the pods on. Scatter over the pine nuts, lemon zest and dill. Using a speed peeler, peel over shavings of parmesan. Drizzle over some olive oil and season with a little flaky sea salt and pepper.

MY FAVOURITE COUSCOUS SALAD

This is my favourite salad to take to BBQ's or for a yummy light lunch. The tomato 'raisins' are the best bit in this salad – they are so deep and rich in flavour and give such a delicious burst of flavour. I much prefer Israeli couscous over the other as this one is more like a pasta and has a really good texture.

3 cups cherry tomatoes, halved
3 tablespoons olive oil
A small bunch thyme
¼ cup olive oil (extra)
2 tablespoons lemon juice
1 teaspoon honey
1 small garlic clove
2 ½ cups Israeli couscous
1 long red chilli, finely diced
½ cup pistachios, chopped
½ cup feta cheese, crumbled
Small bunch chives and flat leaf parsley,
    finely chopped
Optional garnish: Chive flowers

Serves: 5 as a side
Time: Takes time

Preheat the oven to 150°C (300°F). Put the tomatoes on a tray lined with baking paper so they don't stick, single layer and drizzle with olive oil. Season with salt and place thyme sprigs over the top. Roast for 40 minutes. Remove and discard thyme and cook for a further 5–10 minutes. Set aside to cool. In a jar shake the remaining olive oil, lemon juice, honey, garlic and a good pinch of salt and pepper. Set aside. Bring a large pot of water to the boil, salt it well and drop in the couscous. Cook for around 9 minutes, uncovered. Drain and add to a large mixing bowl. While hot, add the dressing and toss well. Take a little of the chilli, feta, pistachios and herbs and set aside to use as a garnish. Toss the rest with the couscous. Fold through the tomatoes. Put onto a serving plate. Top with reserved ingredients. Drizzle with a little extra olive oil, garnish with chive flowers and fresh pepper.

GREEN SALAD

Anytime you feel like you want some tasty vegetables or a nice green salad on the side this is the dish to turn to. So simple and easy to put together.

1 bunch green beans, top end trimmed
1 bunch asparagus, trimmed
2 avocados
Soft herbs – I used a small bunch each of
    tarragon, dill and flat leaf parsley
2 cups rocket, or leafy greens of your
    choice
Olive oil
Juice 1–2 lemons
1 tablespoon black or white sesame seeds
Thyme and borage flowers (optional)

Serves 6 as a side
Time: Easy as

Bring a medium pot of water to the boil. Salt well. Drop in the beans and asparagus and as soon as they are in time for 2 minutes exactly. Cook uncovered. While that is cooking, get a large bowl and fill with some ice and cold water. Once the beans and asparagus have blanched, drain and plunge into the ice water to retain their bright green colour and crunch. When cold, drain and set aside. Scoop out the avocados and quarter. Arrange the avocados, beans and asparagus on a platter or board. Lightly dress the rocket in a bowl with a little olive oil, lemon juice, salt and pepper. Taste. Add more lemon if you like but don't add too much or your leaves will go soggy. Add to the board. I arrange the avocado, beans and asparagus a bit so you can see them. Garnish with the sesame seeds and flowers. Season with a little extra salt and pepper if you wish and an extra drizzle of olive oil.

POTATO SALAD

Such a classic, potato salad. It's a must at barbecues and I love it with southern style fried chicken. I add the beans in there to give a crunch and texture and the herbs give a freshness that I love.

600g (1.3 lbs) potatoes, I used baby Perlas
100g (3.5oz) beans, sliced
250g (9oz) free range streaky bacon
2 spring onions, finely sliced

DRESSING
4 heaped tablespoons mayonnaise
2-3 tablespoons milk
1 teaspoon Dijon mustard
2 tablespoons dill
1 tablespoon flat leaf parsley
1 tablespoon chives

Serves: 6 as a side
Time: A little bit of effort

Heat oven to 200°C (390°F) to fan bake.

Line a tray with baking paper and lay out bacon in a single layer. Cook for around 5–7 minutes until crispy. Cut into bite size pieces and set aside. For the dressing, chop the herbs. Set a little aside to garnish at the end and add the rest to a jar with the remaining dressing ingredients. Shake well to combine. Add a little more milk if needed to thin it out. Season to taste. Cook the beans in boiling salted water for 1 ½ minutes. Drain, and then plunge immediately into a cold ice water bath to retain colour and crunch. Cut the potatoes into bite size pieces and cook in salted boiling water until a knife just goes through the centre with ease, around 10 minutes. Drain and put into a large bowl. I do these last so that you can serve the salad warm if you want. Toss with remaining ingredients. Taste for seasoning. Arrange on a platter. Scatter over remaining herbs and finish with a little extra black pepper.

ROAST POTATOES

The prefect roast potato has an incredibly crunchy outside and soft and fluffy inside, and that's exactly what these are. The key to the perfect roast potato is mostly in selecting the right variety – choose one that is floury not waxy.

1.5kg (3.3lbs) potatoes, all medium size
10 cloves garlic smashed, skins left on
1 handful rosemary
¼ cup olive oil
50g (1.7oz) butter

Serves: 4
Time: Takes time

Preheat oven to 200°C (390°F). Put a large tray into the oven to get hot.

Bring a large pot of water to the boil and salt generously. While that is coming up to heat. Scrub the potatoes with a scrubbing brush keeping the skins on if they are new potoatoes, otherwise, peel them, then cut in half. Boil with the lid on for 8 minutes or until quite soft but not cooked all the way through. Drain thoroughly and give a good shake to rough up. All those fluffy edges are going to give you crispy bits. If a few potatoes break up completely, that's ok. Set aside for now. Take a small pot and heat the oil and the butter together so that its hot and the butter starts to bubble.

Tip out onto the prepared tray. Turn them so that they are all facing cut side down. Take a clean tea towel and press on the tops to squash them all. Drizzle with olive oil, scatter over the majority of rosemary (save a few for garnish) and season with salt. Roast for 1 – 1 ¼ hours in the centre of the oven until crispy and golden. Remove. Discard rosemary. Garnish with reserved rosemary and a little extra salt.

MY MUM'S CHRISTMAS STUFFING ROLLS

This is Mum's signature dish and I have to tell you all, my eldest son was not happy about me sharing this recipe in my book. His exact words were "No, you can't! That's OUR special family recipe. You can't share it with the world!". YES, that is how good this recipe is. The week leading up to Christmas there is a buzz in the family about these stuffing rolls. You know that the stuffing is good when everyone cares more about the stuffing than the actual meat. Every year we ask Mum to make extra, last Christmas she made 180 rolls... between 9 of us! And we ate them all (also good the next day!). Of course, you don't have to serve this just at Christmas time. It goes well as a side dish to any roast meats (but, I would actually happily eat this as a side dish at breakfast even!)

30g (1oz) butter
1 onion, finely diced
1 medium leek, finely diced
2 celery sticks, sliced thinly
100g (3.5oz) smoked ham, diced
50g (1.7oz) parmesan cheese, grated
2 teaspoons Dijon mustard
1 tablespoon dried mixed herbs
3 cups fresh breadcrumbs (made in food
    processor)
1 small free range egg, beaten
500g (1lb) streaky free range bacon

Makes: 40–50
Time: Takes time / If possible,
begin the day before

Melt butter in large frying pan over a medium/high heat and cook the onion, leek, and celery with a pinch of salt and pepper. Cook for 2 minutes then take off the heat. Add the cheese, ham, mustard, and mixed herbs to the cooked mixture and stir well to combine. Then add the breadcrumbs and combine all ingredients with the egg to bind. Cover the mixture and leave to sit in the fridge for 3–4 hours. If possible leave overnight.

Preheat the oven 180°C (350°F). Line a tray with baking paper and set aside.

To make the bacon rolls: Cut rashers of bacon in half and stretch each rasher of bacon (both lengthwise and width). Take a teaspoonful of stuffing mixture and wrap a piece of bacon around each barrel of stuffing and place seam-side down onto the baking paper lined tray. Bake for 20–30 minutes or until crispy and golden.

HOMEMADE MAYONNAISE

Homemade mayonnaise is so easy to make, especially when you use a food processor like I do, but feel free to whisk by hand. I often make mayonnaise as we have 13 chickens so it's a great way to use up the eggs. Some people like to use a mix of olive oil and neutral flavoured oil in mayonnaise – I prefer to keep it just a neutral oil for a light creamy taste, for me olive oil is too strong. Once you have a basic mayo you can keep it plain or add whatever you like to jazz it up. A few options are: a herb mayo – I add 1 cup of tightly packed basil to the egg yolks and give it a good wizz up before adding the oil. To make an aioli – add 1 small clove crushed garlic, more to taste if you like. A preserved lemon and caper mayo – add 2 teaspoons chopped capers and ½ rind of a preserved lemon (or zest of 1 lemon if you don't have preserved lemon) or add things like chipotles or other chillis and hot sauces to serve on fish tacos. So versatile.

4 free range egg yolks
1 tablespoon lemon juice
1 tablespoon rice wine or white wine
   vinegar
1 heaped teaspoon Dijon mustard
1 cup canola oil

In a food processor, add the yolks, lemon juice, vinegar, mustard and season with salt and pepper. Mix up to combine well. With the motor running, SLOWLY pour in the oil. If you add it too quickly it won't get thick and creamy – it will be runny. Once you have added the oil, taste. See if it needs more seasoning. If it's too thick for your liking you can add 1 tablespoon of water and mix again. Store in the fridge for up to a week (no longer as it contains the raw egg yolks)

Makes: 1 cup
Time: Easy as

SALAD DRESSING

This is my most often made salad dressing (apart from a simple lemon juice/olive oil dressing which I also do often). The thing that will change the flavour of this dressing is the vinegar. A few vinegars I have that I use are: red wine, balsamic, rice wine vinegar, chardonnay vinegar, raspberry red wine, or I sometimes use the juice from the jar of gherkins as it's vinegary with a pickle flavour, yum!

¼ cup good olive oil
1 tablespoon lemon juice
1 tablespoon vinegar
1 heaped teaspoon Dijon mustard
1 level teaspoon runny honey (or castor
   sugar)

Shake all the ingredients together in a jar. Taste to see if you need to adjust the seasoning. I like to make double, even triple this recipe, especially in the summer months, for an easy to grab and use dressing. Will keep in the fridge for a week.

Makes: Enough for one salad
Time: Easy as

Preserves

The one thing that my brothers and I remember most about our Gran, even my cousins who are based on the other side of the world in Dublin will say the same thing – her preserves, especially her peaches! A food memory I have of my Gran is standing beside her on a stool in her kitchen, I was maybe 4 years old, her peeling peaches to preserve and I would eat the furry skins as she would peel. She had rows and rows of glass jars filled with an assortment of homemade preserves, all lined up proudly on the shelves in the laundry. She would make her own chutneys, relish (her relish recipe is in this section) spaghetti – like canned spaghetti but a homemade version, and pickled beetroot. Every Sunday she would on request fry some cold boiled potatoes in oil and we would eat them hot with the purple pickled beetroot. The combination of vinegar from the beets and fried potatoes was incredible. It made going to Sunday school at their church, in itchy wool stockings and pretty dresses, (I was a tomboy so it was the worst thing for me) worth it knowing we were going to get that lunch after.

Because of this childhood memory I now have a connection and attraction as an adult to preserving. So it was inevitable that I would continue my Gran's tradition. I love that we can jar a season and enjoy it in other months. Preserving is not complicated; marmalade is probably the hardest thing in this chapter. All you have to do is ensure you have sterilised jars, this stops bacteria forming when you are keeping something for a long period of time. To do this I simply preheat oven to 150°C (300°F), wash the jars in hot soapy water and rinse well, then place the jars onto a baking tray and put in the oven until they are completely dry. Lids can go in the oven too if they don't have rubber seals. If they do have rubber, boil in a large pot of water otherwise they will melt in the oven. It is important to fill the jars and seal your jars while your preserves are still hot to prevent bugs and bacteria.

The Forest Cantina

tomato relish

tomato relish

GRAN'S TOMATO RELISH

We always love to have a relish in the fridge. To have with cheese sandwiches, to serve with things like quiche or homemade sausage rolls – it is the perfect accompaniment. If you make it out of tomato season you can use tinned tomatoes which is what I have used here. This is my Grandmother's recipe that I have adapted slightly.

4x 400g (14oz) tins chopped tomatoes (or 1.6kg/3.5lb fresh tomatoes)
1 cup white wine vinegar
1 ¼ cup FairTrade unrefined sugar
6 onions, diced
2 large apples, grated
½ cup raisins
1 tablespoon mustard powder
1 tablespoon hot curry powder
Pinch cayenne pepper (more if you like it really hot)
2 tablespoons salt
2 teaspoons pepper

Makes: 7 cups
Time: A little bit of effort

Sterilise jars and lids. In a large heavy bottom pot, add all of the ingredients and bring to the boil. Once boiling, reduce to a medium/low heat and cook for around 30 minutes. The pectin in the apples will thicken the relish. Once the relish is cooked and it's nice and glossy and thick, ladle into hot sterilised jars.

PICKLED CUCUMBERS

I usually serve these with a curry, the sharp sweet and sour flavour and the crunch goes so well with curry. It's a wonderful contrast. You can use them in burgers or sandwiches or with cheese and crackers. In Japan they use pickled cucumber as an accompaniment to sushi and rice. It is so easy to make – the thing that takes the most time is the cooling of the syrup. You want to make sure the syrup is completely refrigerator cold before adding the cucumbers so they retain their crunch. If the liquid is hot it will cook the cucumbers.

1 cup rice wine vinegar
1 cup FairTrade unrefined sugar
1 long cucumber

Makes: 1 large jar, depending on the size of your cucumber
Time: Easy as / takes time for the syrup to cool however

In a medium sized pot over a medium/high heat combine the vinegar and sugar, stirring until the sugar has dissolved. Cool completely and put in the fridge to get really cold. Meanwhile, cut the cucumber in half and then in half lengthwise. With a teaspoon, scrape the seeds out of the cucumber, then cut into half-moon shapes. Add to the syrup. Will keep in the fridge for 2 days, but I think they are best eaten the day they are made for its best crunchy texture.

PRESERVED LEMONS

A tiny little jar of these is so expensive in the shops. The reason being because you have to leave them for 3 months before using them. A little inconvenient, but they are worth the wait. So I make the biggest jar I can find when I do so that it's worth the time invested in these. When I first had preserved lemons, I used part of the pith and it was so disgusting, it tasted like soap. So what I do when I use these now is completely remove all the inner part and rinse under water to remove everything except the yellow rind. And it is amazing! Use in salads, dressings and, of course, Moroccan dishes – anywhere where it calls for lemon zest, try swapping it for preserved lemon. It's such a delicate and unusual lemon flavour.

12–15 organic lemons
300g Kosher or flaky sea salt
Optional additions: 2 bay leaves,
*   2 cinnamon sticks, 2 dried chillies*

Makes: 1 large preserving jar
Feel free to half this recipe
Time: Easy as to make / takes 3 months
to preserve
Lasts: Over a year in the fridge

Sterilise a large jar. Wash and scrub the lemons. Put a jug of water on to boil. The classic Moroccan way is to cut each lemon in quarters but not right through, so that the pieces are still attached at the stem end, and to stuff each with a tablespoon of salt and squeeze it closed. Do this one at a time and place into a jar as you go. Continue and repeat until the jar is full of lemons (pressing down and compacting them as you go). If there is any salt left tip it in. If you are using any bay, cinnamon or chillies – poke those in too. Top up with boiled water (to sterilise) so everything is completely covered. Seal and date the jar and wait 3 months!

LEMON CURD

My husband adores lemon curd and his Mum made it often for him growing up. He likes it on toast, I like it on chewy bagels with cream cheese. A few other ways you can use it are to fold it through yoghurt and serve with muesli (see my homemade muesli recipe on page 27), eat with crepes or pancakes, fill a sweet baked tart shell with curd – mini ones for a canapé and top with whipped cream, use as a filling in donuts, top pavlovas with cream, curd and berries, soften some store bought vanilla ice cream – ripple through some lemon curd and refreeze. These are just some delicious ways to inspire you how to use curd. Or just eat by the spoonful!

1 ½ cup (330g /12 oz) FairTrade unrefined
*   sugar*
4 free range eggs
Plus an extra 4 egg yolks
Zest of 2 lemons
¾ – 1 cup fresh lemon juice
160g (5.6 oz) butter, chilled and cubed

Makes: 3 medium sized jars
Time: Easy as

Sterilise jars and lids. In a medium sized pot, whisk together the sugar, eggs and extra egg yolks so they are combined well then whisk in the zest and lemon juice. Add the butter and warm over a medium/low heat, whisking continuously until all the butter is melted. Then switch to a wooden spoon and stir until thickened, around 10 minutes. To test if it is done – dip the wooden spoon in the curd, on the back of the spoon run your finger through it to make a line. If the line keeps its shape, without the sides running, it is ready. The curd will set more when it is cold. Pour hot curd into sterilised jars.

To store: Keep lemon curd in the fridge and use within 2 weeks.

RASPBERRY JAM

There couldn't be anything more traditional in my Mum's house the week before Christmas than her making raspberry jam for gifts with Mariah Carey's Christmas album playing on repeat in the background. Just the thought of the two things together makes me smile. Jam is so easy to make, especially when you follow the rule of thumb – 1kg fruit to 1kg sugar. And I use jam setting sugar for a guaranteed easy set. Whether you are making homemade gifts or stocking your larder, jam is easier to make than you may think – so have a go. Check out my labelling page at the back of the book for how I make my own labels.

1kg (2.2 lbs) raspberries (frozen or fresh)
1Kg (2.2 lbs) jam setting sugar
1 knob butter

Makes: 4–5 medium sized jars
Time: Easy

Put a plate (metal) in the freezer. Sterilise jars and lids (see the chapter introduction page 143 on how to do that).

Mix the berries and sugar together over a medium/low heat until the sugar has dissolved. Once dissolved, add butter and bring to a rapid boil and time 4 minutes. Take off the heat. Do the 'wrinkle' test by putting a spoon of the jam onto the cold plate. Wait until it cools then push with your finger. If it wrinkles it's ready. If not, put pot back on the heat and then cool for a further 2 minutes testing again. Ladle hot jam into hot sterilised jars.

GRAN'S MARMALADE

Marmalade requires a little more time and skill than jam making. This recipe came from my Grandmother's hand-written recipe book. Her recipe books are a little cryptic at times with instructions like "chop fruit, cook until set". Obviously she knew what she meant, and because she passed away when I was 10 years old I couldn't ask "did you remove the peel first and finely chop? Did you juice the fruit and then chop? How long did you cook it for?"... so I had to do a bit of recipe testing, cooking this several times from her basic recipe to come up with some instructions below that are easy to follow. It does take a long time to reduce and boil down, but it does work and has delicious results. This marmalade also makes a delicious glaze for a Christmas ham.

4 grapefruit
2 oranges
2 lemons
3.5 litres water (15 cups)
9 cups (2kg / 4.4lbs) sugar

Makes: 11 cups (it reduces quite a bit from the 15 cups of water added)
Time: Takes time

Sterilise jars and lids. Peel all the rind off the fruit with a speed peeler and set aside. Cut the bottom off the fruit so that it sits flat on the board, and cut all the white pith off the fruit and discard it. Squeeze the juice from the fruit into a large heavy bottom pot. Chop all the fruit flesh (a medium dice) discarding any membrane and seeds. Add to the pot. Take the rind of the fruit and stack on top of each other and slice finely, into 3cm (1 inch) long shreds. Add to pot with the water and sugar. Cook, stirring occasionally, over a medium/low heat until the sugar has dissolved then increase the heat and bring to a rapid boil, cooking for around 1 hour, skimming off any scum that comes to the surface and being careful it doesn't boil over. It is ready when it is thick and glossy and slightly reduced. It might look slightly runny but it does thicken once it has been jarred and cools completely. Ladle the hot marmalade into hot sterilised jars and lids.

VANILLA SUGAR

Vanilla pods are a decadent and expensive product, and if you love baking and making desserts, I'm sure you would have used these many times before. This page is to inspire, rather than being all about the recipes. There are different ways of making vanilla sugar, some people like to process the sugar and the beans together, but because I use the pods in vanilla extract, I like to 'perfume' sugar instead. When buying vanilla beans, instead of keeping them in the pack they come in, store them in a jar with some sugar until you are ready to use them. It will give the sugar the yummiest vanilla scent, which, you can use in place of regular sugar for baking and desserts.

You can use as much or as little sugar and pods as you want, obviously the more pods you have the stronger the vanilla will be. I also top the sugar up as I use it and replace with fresh beans when they have been used.

1 large jar for sugar
6 cups FairTrade unrefined sugar
5 vanilla pods

Time: Easy as

Half fill your jar of sugar then put your pods in. Cover with more sugar to the top. Screw the lid on and let it sit until you are ready to use a pod.

VANILLA EXTRACT

The difference between vanilla essence and vanilla extract is that essence is artificially made to taste like vanilla and contains lots of chemicals to do so. It is fake tasting, and I personally don't like either the flavour or the smell. Extract is pure vanilla from vanilla beans steeped in alcohol (over 35% alcohol) and that's it. Lots of recipes will use vanilla pods with the seeds too, which will give you a really beautiful and strong extract. I prefer to use the seeds in a dessert or something like that and use the scraped leftover pods instead – and it works just as well. Even if I have made a crème anglaise with pods, I will wash, then airdry them and use them in extract. You can use any alcohol you like over 35% – rum, bourbon or whisky. I prefer to use vodka as it doesn't have a strong flavour so the flavour of the vanilla really shines.

200ml alcohol (or you can make small
  bottles or much larger)
3 used vanilla pods

Time: Easy to make / takes 8 weeks to extract

Sterilise a jar or bottle of your choice. Pour in the alcohol and add the pods. Shake well and let it sit for about 2 months – shaking the jar or bottle once a week if possible to mix it all up. You know it is ready when the smell is strong with vanilla and the colour is dark (which is good when you use a white sprit so you can see that colour change). Wherever a recipe says to use a teaspoon of vanilla essence or extract, just take a teaspoon from your jar.

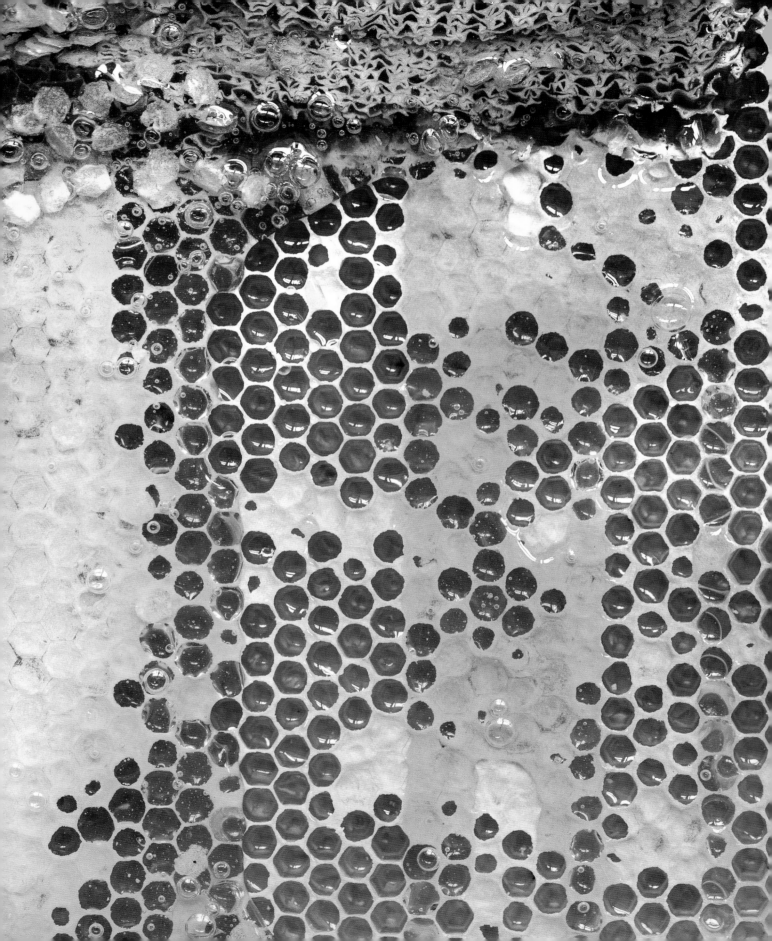

Sweet treats

Oh man, do I love sweet endings? YES I DO! Like most things I make, they are extreme opposites – easy or incredibly time consuming. Like an apple crumble, made in minutes, takes a little while to bake in the oven but it's served hot with some store-bought vanilla ice cream – so simple. That hot/cold combination is a dream! Or when I am in the mood for some serious dessert making, like my raspberry mousse cakes that have many different elements and textures, they require a lot of patience and attention – but I just love putting effort into something that gets "ooooo's and aaaaa's" from the people I serve it to.

I also love baking, cakes and biscuits are my favourite. All my favourite recipes are in this section as well as my Fair Trade Chocolate cake. Through my book I have used fair trade ingredients and I won in 2013 the Big Fair Bake competition with my creation. It showcases lots of fair trade ingredients and my love for supporting Fair Trade.

Chocolate has to be my number one – especially a really good quality real trade single origin chocolate with goodness in both flavour and the story behind it. The chocolate mousse cake in this section could be the last thing I ever eat and I'd be happy! Big call I know, but if you are a chocolate lover too, that won't disappoint. I find if people aren't so keen on chocolate (apparently those people actually exist!) they usually love lemon or fruity desserts. And there are plenty of those within this chapter too! Enjoy.

HONEY CAKE WITH VANILLA BEAN FROSTING, FRESH FIGS AND HONEY WALNUTS

If you are looking for a cake with a more unusual flavour profile, this is it. My husband adores it – a beekeeper's cake. Depending on what type of honey you use it will affect the flavour of the cake. I made this during the manuka flower season, so our bee hives were full of this strong, dark amber honey making the cake really strong with honey.

1 cup (250g/8oz) butter, softened
1 cup (225g/7oz) FairTrade unrefined sugar
4 free range eggs
3 cups flour
2 teaspoons baking powder
1 cup milk
⅔ cup runny honey
Juice of 1 medium sized lemon
1 teaspoon vanilla paste or extract

FOR THE HONEY WALNUTS
140g (5oz) walnuts
2 tablespoons honey

FOR THE VANILLA BEAN FROSTING
1 cup butter (250g/8oz) room temperature
3 cups (450g/15oz) icing sugar
3-4 teaspoons vanilla bean paste
2 tablespoons milk

TO SERVE
Fresh figs (I used 3 large and 5 small)
Vanilla bean yoghurt to serve
A little extra honey to drizzle

Makes: Serves 12–16 depending on the size of slices
Time: Takes time / I begin the day before

Preheat the oven to 180°C (350°F). Line the base of a 21cm (8 inch) round cake tin with baking paper. Grease the sides with butter then dust over the butter with flour and set aside. In a stand mixer (or by hand) cream the butter and the sugar together until light and fluffy. Add the eggs one at a time until incorporated well after each addition. Sieve the flour and the baking powder together and add to the creamed butter and sugar. Combine in a large jug the milk, honey, lemon juice and vanilla and whisk well to combine. Add to the mixing bowl and then mix gently until everything is just combined. Don't overmix or the cake will be tough. Pour into prepared cake tin and bake for 1–1¼ hours, rotating tin once, or until a skewer comes out clean when inserted into the centre. Cool in the tin then remove and transfer to a wire rack. Once completely cool, split the cake in half by cutting with a bread knife.

For the walnuts: While the oven is hot, on a tray lined with baking paper, spread out the walnuts and drizzle over the honey. Bake for 5 minutes. Remove and toss the walnuts through the melted honey and return to the oven for 4 minutes longer. Set aside to cool. When cool, chop half the nuts and leave the other half whole.

For the frosting: In a stand mixer, beat the butter for a minute on its own then add the icing sugar, vanilla paste and milk and beat for around 5 minutes until fluffy. When the cake is completely cooled, invert the dome top part of the cake so that it is on the bottom of the cake stand. Fill cake with half the frosting and spread out evenly with a palate knife. Top with the other cake half, the flat part of the cake on top and cover with the remaining frosting, spreading down and around the sides. Once the frosting has been evenly spread out over the cake, clean your palate knife and warm it under hot water, dry the knife and while it is still hot, smooth the frosting out to get a nice clean finish on the cake. At this point I chill the cake overnight or at least for 4 hours so that the slices of cake are really neat and clean when cut. But you can skip this step if you are not fussed.

Once frosted and ready to serve, top with walnuts and then with sliced figs. When you go to serve a slice, cut the cake and serve the figs on the side with a little drizzle of honey over the top and a spoonful of yoghurt to go with it.

FAIR TRADE CHOCOLATE CAKE

Throughout my book I talk about and use Fair Trade products, and this cake is a real celebration of those wonderful consciously sourced products. I am incredibly proud of this delicious cake. It does take a bit of time and work, but it is the perfect cake for a special occasion.

1 tablespoon instant FairTrade coffee
    granules (or fair trade espresso coffee
    of your choice)
¾ cup water
2 cups FairTrade unrefined sugar
1¾ cups plain flour
¾ cup FairTrade organic cocoa powder
2 teaspoons vanilla paste or extract
2 teaspoons baking soda
1 teaspoon baking powder
½ teaspoon salt
2 free range eggs
1¼ cups milk
½ cup melted coconut oil (or canola oil)

FOR THE CHOCOLATE
BUTTERCREAM

4 tablespoons warm milk
4 tablespoons FairTrade cocoa
200g (3½ oz) butter, at room temperature
3 cups icing sugar

FOR THE GANACHE

1 cup cream
250g (8oz) chocolate (I used Real Trade
    organic 70%)
30g (1oz) butter

TO DECORATE

1 punnet raspberries
Chocolate pearls

Serves: 12–16 depending on the size of slices
Time: Takes time / begin the day before

Note: I make and fill the cake the day before and let it sit in the fridge overnight. By chilling the cake the buttercream sets and you get perfect smooth layers when you cut through the cake.

Preheat the oven to 180°C (350°F). Grease and line the base of a 23cm (9 inch) cake tin with baking paper. Butter and flour the sides and set aside. Dissolve the coffee granules in water, then place all ingredients into a food processor and process until well combined and smooth. Pour the runny mixture into the cake tin. Bake in the preheated oven for 40–45 minutes, or until a skewer inserted into the centre of the cake comes out clean. If it's not quite cooked – set a timer and check every 2–3 minutes after that. When completely cool – slice dome off the top of the cake and flip the cake onto a cake plate – cut side down (so the cake is now flipped, the bottom of the cake is now the top). Slice the cake in half with a bread knife. Set aside while you make the buttercream.

For the buttercream: Dissolve the cocoa in the warm milk to make a smooth thick paste, allow to cool so it doesn't melt the buttercream. Beat the butter and icing sugar together until it is pale and fluffy in texture. Beat in the cooled chocolate mixture. Thin with extra milk if needed. Remove the top part of the cake and fill the centre with buttercream. Smooth out with a palate knife to the edges. Put the other half of the cake on top and press gently. Take a clean knife and run around the edge of the cake to remove excess buttercream from the sides so that it is smooth and flush to the cake. Cover in plastic wrap and chill overnight in the fridge.

For the ganache: Cut chocolate into chunks and set aside. Heat the cream until it almost reaches boiling point then remove from the heat. Put chocolate and butter into the hot cream and leave for 2–3 minutes without stirring, then whisk well. Put the ganache in the fridge until it has firmed up a little, so it's not runny when you top the cake – I left mine for about 40 minutes – stirring a few times. Don't let it harden too much, just enough so that it's like a smooth frosting rather than a liquid.

Putting the cake together: I ganache my cake on a clean dry bench and transfer it back to the cake plate with two fish flips – so the plate doesn't get too messy. Completely cover the top of the cake with some ganache and bring down and around the sides. Use a clean palatte knife to smooth the ganache. Decorate the cake with raspberries around the edge and a few chocolate pearls inside. I serve slices that are 2 raspberries wide. It is a full-on cake, so a slither is perfect.

LEMON YOGHURT CAKE

I baked this pretty cake in my thrifted bundt tin – it's a really large tin holding a lot of cake batter! So feel free to half this recipe, or it would easily make 2 loaf tins which is what lemon yoghurt cake is often made in. I made this cake on a large scale to take full advantage of the tins pretty pattern all the way from the top to the bottom edge, and I just love the simple lemon icing on top, dripping down like a snow capped mountain. I have to admit something though, in case when you come to add the blueberries and wonder how mine stayed sitting so neatly – I used toothpicks on a few to hold them in place. I wanted to let you know that, because I got so frustrated that they would not stay. So that was my solution (and food styling tip) for you all.

2 cups plain unsweetened yoghurt
2 cups FairTrade unrefined sugar
6 free range eggs
Zest of 2 large lemons
2 teaspoons vanilla paste
1 cup neutral flavoured oil (I used canola)
3 cups flour
4 teaspoons baking powder
⅔ cup fresh lemon juice
Cooking spray

FOR THE ICING
¾ cup icing sugar
Juice 2–3 medium lemons

TO SERVE
1 punnet blueberries
Edible flowers – I used black violas and
  violet cornflower petals

Serves: 12–14
Time: Takes time

Preheat oven to 180°C (350°F). Spray your tin with cooking spray and then dust with flour. Bang out excess into sink. Set aside. In a mixer with a paddle attachment (or in a large mixing bowl, you can mix by hand) mix the yoghurt, sugar, eggs, zest and vanilla paste together until fully combined. Add the oil and mix well again. Then add the lemon juice and mix well. By doing the mixing in this step it will stop the mix from curdling. Lastly fold through the flour and baking powder – don't overmix otherwise your cake will be tough. Pour into the prepared tin and bake in the centre of the oven for 1 hour or until a skewer comes out clean when inserted into the centre. If baking two loaves, test after 45 minutes to see if the cake is cooked. Once cooked, allow to cool in the tin for 10 minutes.

To demould, I took a paring knife and loosened the crispy bits that were stuck to the edge of the tin, inverted onto a cake plate holding tin with tea towel and the bottom of the plate and giving the cake two firm shakes. If this process doesn't work the first time, go back and check the sides of the tin with a knife and shake again.

For the icing and serving: Mix the icing sugar with lemon juice. If you want a thick icing like mine – don't add too much lemon juice, just enough to make a paste. It might look like it's too thick – but a paste consistency is what you want. If it's too runny – it will be more like a glaze, it will be transparent rather than being white and will drop off the cake rather than holding the drip shapes. Decorate cake with blueberries and edible flowers.

OAT CHOCOLATE CHIP COOKIES

We love these cookies in our house – they are a favourite for the lunch box too and keep well in an air tight container. Perfect for dipping into hot chocolates or for serving with milk. They are also the traditional 'Santa' cookie that I make each year. I must warn you though, these cookies disappear fast, so you could double the recipe to make them last a little longer.

160g (5.7oz) butter, softened
1 firmly packed cup (200g/7oz) brown
  sugar
1 egg
1 teaspoon vanilla extract
1 cup (150g/5.5oz) flour
1 teaspoon baking powder
2 cups (230g/8oz) rolled oats
1 cup (190g/6.7oz) chocolate chips

Makes: 24
Time: A little bit of effort

Preheat oven to 180°C (350°F). Line 2 large baking trays with baking paper. Cream the butter and the sugar together until it's creamy, light and fluffy. Add the egg and the vanilla and beat well. Fold in the flour, oats and chocolate chips until combined. Roll heaped tablespoon size portions into balls, I fit 12 per tray – they don't spread too much, so place about 2cm (¾in) apart. Once they are all rolled out, flatten with a fork dipped in flour to help it from sticking.

Bake for 15–20 minutes until they are golden brown. Leave to cool on the tray for 5 minutes before removing to a wire rack. Store in an airtight container.

AFGHANS

This is my all-time favourite biscuit. Traditionally it is topped with an icing made from cocoa and icing sugar, but I prefer melting chocolate – a good Fair Trade dark chocolate, and dipping each biscuit in. Afghans are usually topped with a walnut, but I like mine with a coconut garnish.

400g (14oz) butter, softened
1 cup (8oz) FairTrade unrefined sugar
2 ½ (13oz) cups flour
½ cup (4oz) cocoa
3 (4oz) cups cornflakes, crushed lightly
  with your hands
200g (7oz) FairTrade chocolate (I used
  single origin 70%)
¼ cup coconut chips
15 walnut halves

Makes: 30
Time: Takes time

Preheat oven to 180°C (350°F) and line 2 trays with baking paper.
Cream butter and sugar together until light and fluffy. Add the flour, cocoa and cornflakes and mix until just combined. Take heaped tablespoons of mix and roll into balls, shaping and pressing together with your hands. Flatten tops of the biscuit slightly with your fingers and if the sides of the biscuit crack from doing this, push back into shape so they don't crumble when they bake. Bake for 15–20 minutes. Cool on the tray for 5 minutes before removing to a cooling rack.

To melt the chocolate, take a large pot and fill it a quarter of the way with hot water and bring to a simmer over a medium heat. Break the chocolate up and add to a heatproof bowl big enough to sit over the pot of water. The steam from the water will melt the chocolate in the bowl above gently without burning the chocolate. Once most of the chocolate has melted, give it a stir with a wooden spoon, the melted chocolate should melt the rest. When it has all melted, remove from the heat.

Dip each biscuit into the chocolate. Top with a walnut or coconut, I did half and half. Once chocolate has set, store in an airtight container.

BRANDY SNAPS

My grandmother left this recipe written in one of her books and it's the one thing that my dad talks about her making. A special thing about this recipe is that I actually have my Gran's brandy snap horns which I use to make these. If you don't have horns, you can make more of a 'cannelloni' shape by rolling them around the end of wooden spoon. Keep an eye out in thrift stores for horns, I often see them around, really cheap. This is such a lovely old-fashioned recipe which we love to have at Christmas. Filled with soft, whipped cream they are a nostalgic favourite for generations within my family.

100g (3.5oz) butter, diced
1/3 cup golden syrup
½ cup FairTrade unrefined sugar
½ cup flour
1 teaspoon ginger
½ teaspoon cinnamon

TO SERVE
Softly whipped cream sweetened with a
*   little icing sugar*

Makes 24
Time: Takes time / Can only bake 2 per tray so takes time to get through all the mixture

Preheat oven to 180°C (350°F) and line 2 trays with baking paper.

In a medium sized pot heat over a medium/high heat, warm the butter, golden syrup and sugar in a pot until the butter is melted and the sugar is dissolved, stirring occasionally.

Meanwhile in a mixing bowl, with a whisk, mix the flour, ginger, and cinnamon together. When the butter mixture is melted and dissolved, pour into the flour, whisking constantly until you have a smooth batter. You can use the batter right away but it's easier to portion and work with once it's sat for a bit to harden a little to look like caramel.

The brandy snaps spread quite a bit so space them apart and bake two at a time, per tray. Take a heaped teaspoon of mixture and place on the prepared tray, I cook 4 at a time, two on each tray. That is the best number to bake as when they come out you have to work rather quickly rolling them before they harden to shape them.

Bake for 7–8 minutes until a dark brown colour. Once baked, remove from the oven and let them sit for about 1 minute (as they are too soft to work with immediately after coming from the oven). To roll, I place a horn on top of the flat brandy snap and using a palatte knife fold the edge over the horn and use my hand to roll the brandy snap around the horn and the palatte knife to help guide the actual brandy snap around the horn. Once it's rolled to a cone shape, I pick it up and give the edge a press on the bench to seal it closed.

Leave to cool on the horn. Pull them off carefully by twisting them just before the next ones are ready to come out of the oven. Repeat until they are all finished. They will keep for a few days, unfilled in an air tight container. I usually make these the day before I want to use them. When ready to serve fill with whipped cream.

PEACH MELBA RICE PUDDING

When I was pregnant I would crave coconut milk rice pudding – and I had to have it a VERY specific way ... nice and creamy, definitely not 'solid', almost a risotto consistency. Post pregnancy I was tired of plain rice pudding so decided to jazz it up. I combined two classics – peach melba and rice pudding together and it is such a dreamy combination! There are some adjustments that you can make here. If you are not obsessed with coconut cream like I am, just use the same quantity of regular cream and maybe a little extra sugar to taste (as coconut cream is sweet). Also, if you want a cheats version – use canned sliced peaches and a little raspberry jam for a faster option. Just as delicious.

FOR THE PEACHES

1 cup FairTrade unrefined sugar

3 cups water

6 fresh peaches (I used Golden Queens, but the white flesh ones are pretty too)

FOR THE RASPBERRY COULIS

½ cup frozen or fresh raspberries

2 tablespoons FairTrade unrefined sugar

1 teaspoon lemon juice

FOR THE RICE PUDDING

1 cup Arborio rice

400ml (14oz) tin FairTrade coconut cream

400ml (14oz) tin filled up with milk

⅓ cup FairTrade unrefined sugar

1 ½ tablespoons cornflour

2 teaspoons vanilla paste

TO SERVE

Grated or shaved white chocolate

Serves: 6

Time: Takes time / Rice must be soaked for at least 1 hour

Put the rice into a bowl and cover with water and let it soak for at least an hour or overnight. By soaking the rice, it means it will cook faster.

Poaching the peaches: Put the water and sugar in a medium pot, big enough to fit the peaches in and bring to the boil. Once boiling, turn down to a simmer. Cut a little cross in the bottoms of the peaches to help peel off the skin later. Cover and simmer gently for 15–20 minutes until tender but not overly soft. Remove and set aside. Once cool enough to handle, peel and discard skin.

While the peaches are cooking make your coulis. Bring the raspberries and sugar to the boil. Simmer, stirring occasionally for about 15 minutes until it thickens slightly. Strain and press through a sieve to remove seeds. Stir in the lemon juice.

When ready to cook the rice pudding, drain rice and add to a large pot with the coconut cream, milk and sugar. Cook over a medium heat for about 12 minutes stirring often, like you would a risotto (if you don't soak the rice – this step could take 30 minutes). Turn down to a medium/low heat if it's cooking too quickly. To know if it's done, taste some of the rice to see if it's cooked. To thicken, mix in a small cup the cornflour and equal parts of cold water together to dissolve. Add to the rice pudding and stir for about 1 minute to cook and thicken. Fold through your vanilla paste.

To serve scoop between bowls (or glasses if you want to get fancy) top with a poached peach, pour over some of the raspberry coulis and top with some white chocolate.

APPLE CRUMBLE

This is my mother-in-law Judy's crumble that I adapted slightly to make it my own. Judy freezes crumble topping for an quick go-to dessert. You could double the topping you need, using half now, and half another day. The thing that I love most about this recipe is the unpeeled grated apple – genius! It's so fast to prepare and the grated apple ensures that the apple will be cooked all the way through. Serve with all the works on the side. Crème anglaise, runny cream and vanilla ice cream. Got to have ice cream – that hot pudding, cold creamy ice cream combo is a winner.

¾ cup rolled oats
¾ cup FairTrade unrefined sugar
½ cup flour
½ cup organic coconut chips (or
    desiccated coconut)
1 teaspoon FairTrade cinnamon
½ teaspoon mixed spice
75g (3 oz) butter, soft but not melted
6 apples (I used 4 Granny Smith and
    2 Braeburn)

Serves 6
Time: Quick preparation but slow
cooking

Preheat oven to 180°C (350°F).

Mix the dry ingredients, the oats, sugar, flour, coconut, cinnamon and mixed spice together in a bowl. Rub in the butter with your fingertips so that you have a nice crumb.

Grate the apples, washed and unpeeled and put into an oven proof dish discarding the core and seeds. Cover with the crumble and bake for 45 minutes or until golden. Serve with your favourite accompaniments.

CRÈME ANGLAISE

This is the French version of an English custard and it's slightly runnier, which I prefer. It's the perfect accompaniment to hot, wintery puddings. (see my labelling page 195 at the back of the book for my tips on how to 'put a label on it').

2 cups milk
4 free range egg yolks
⅓ cup FairTrade unrefined sugar
2 teaspoons cornflour
1 teaspoon vanilla paste or 1 vanilla pod

Makes: 2 cups
Time: Easy as

Heat the milk in a pot over a medium/high heat until hot but not boiling. While that is coming up to heat whisk the eggs, sugar, cornflour and vanilla (if using a pod, split it, and scrape the seeds) in a bowl. Add a third of the milk to the yolk mixture to begin with, whisking well, and then add the rest of the milk while continuously whisking.

Pour the custard back into the pot that you warmed the milk in and cook over a medium heat stirring until it thickens. You want to remove it when it's just thick enough, if you over cook it, it will curdle and go lumpy. It might seem like it needs longer to cook – but it will thicken more when it cools. To test if it's ready take a metal spoon and dip it into the crème anglaise. On the back of the spoon, run your finger through the middle to make a line. If it holds its shape and the sides don't run to the center, it's ready. If you over cook it – it can curdle and have an 'eggy' flavour. Pour immediately into a jug (or a milk bottle) so it stops it cooking.

MY CHRISTMAS PANETTONE PUDDING

The fact that we only eat this once a year makes this dessert not only traditional, but also something to look forward to. Panettone (a sweet Italian loaf with origins from Milan) is available at Christmas – so unless you made your own, you could only make this in the month of December. I have been making this dessert for about 8 years now and it's a family favourite. I just love a pudding that is hot and comforting with all the trimmings to go with it. This is a 'bread and butter pudding' with a festive twist.

1 large panettone loaf (or two small ones)
50g (1.7oz) butter, melted
¼ cup FairTrade unrefined sugar
1 teaspoon cinnamon

FOR THE CUSTARD
1 cup cream
1 teaspoon vanilla paste or a vanilla pod
   split
½ cups FairTrade unrefined sugar
9 free range eggs

TO SERVE
Crème angalise (page 169)
Vanilla bean ice cream

Serves: 8
Time: A little bit of effort

Heat oven to 180°C (350°F) and grease an oven proof dish with butter and set aside.

Slice the brown top, sides and bottom off the loaf not taking off too much of the inside, discard (or eat). The reason I take these bits off is that I feel they go too dark when baked. Cut the loaf into 2cm (1 inch) dices. In a large bowl toss the panettone with the melted butter, sugar and cinnamon and mix well. Put into the prepared dish and set aside while you make the custard.

For the custard: Warm the cream, vanilla (if using a pod, scrape seeds out and add the seeds and the pod to the mix) and sugar together in a medium sized pot. You want to heat it to almost boiling, but don't let it completely come to the boil or you will scald the cream. While that is coming up to heat, in a bowl whisk the eggs. Slowly pour the hot cream mixture a little at a time into the eggs, continually whisking so that it doesn't cook and scramble the eggs. Pour over the cubed panettone.

To bake: Cook in a bain marie (water bath) so the pudding cooks evenly and gently. To do this put the dish with the pudding inside a larger roasting dish. Pour hot water around the pudding dish so it comes halfway up the outside of the dish, being careful not to get any water in the actual pudding. Bake for 30–35 minutes or until the custard has set in the middle and it's golden and crunchy on top.

Serve hot with crème angalise and ice cream.

GINGER BEER AND HONEY POACHED PEARS

I like using ginger beer to poach pears as it imparts a lovely flavour and is also family friendly (as opposed to poaching in wine). The cooking timing depends on the ripeness of the pear, mine were soft and juicy but not mushy, and also coring the pears mean they cook faster too. And coring the pears makes them so much nicer to eat as you can simply dig in and eat the entire thing without having to eat around the core, a little bit of effort in the prep time is worth it in the end. This dessert may look a little fancy, but all I did was take a sheet of puff pastry and some good quality store-bought vanilla bean ice cream to jazz up this fruity dessert. It's not too sweet or overly heavy, just a cute little ending to a meal.

1.5 litres (6 cups) ginger beer

1 cup FairTrade unrefined sugar

3 tablespoons honey

1 cinnamon stick

2 thumb size pieces of ginger, skin on sliced

6 pears (Bosc are a good variety for poaching as they are firmer but I used the d'anjou pears here)

1 sheet flaky pastry, butterpuff if you can find it

2 tablespoons icing sugar

Serves: 5
Time: A little bit of effort

Preheat oven to 200°C (390°F) on fan bake.

In a medium pot that will fit the pears snuggly, over a medium heat, warm the ginger beer, sugar, honey, cinnamon and ginger together stirring occasionally until the sugar dissolves then bring to a simmer. While that is happening, peel your pears leaving the stalks. Core your pears with an apple corer, or, use a paring knife and a teaspoon to cut then scrape the core and seeds out. Put the pears into the simmering ginger beer and time for 15 minutes. The pears are ready when a paring knife can go through the centre with ease. Remove with a slotted spoon to a plate.

To make a syrup: Scoop out and discard the cinnamon and ginger. Pour the liquid into a large heat proof jug then take 2 cups of the liquid and put back into the pot and bring to the boil. Boil and reduce by half until you have a thick syrup about the same consistency as runny honey (about 10 minutes) Set aside.

TIP: Any spare syrup can be frozen and made into popsicles.

For the pastry: Cut out 5 circles of pastry bigger than the base of your pear (I used a mason jar lid). Line a flat tray with baking paper and put the pastry circles on, followed by another sheet of baking paper and another flat tray to weigh the pastry down. This stops the pastry from over puffing – you'll get a flat, yet crisp and flaky base for your pears if you do this method. Bake for 10 minutes on the second to top shelf in the oven, then check the pastry. It should be golden and evenly cooked. Remove and set aside.

To plate: Place a pastry circle on a plate and dust with icing sugar. Put a pear on top and a scoop of vanilla bean ice cream on the side. Spoon around the ginger beer syrup. Serve.

COCONUT PANNA COTTA WITH A TROPICAL FRUIT SALSA

Panna cotta is one of those recipes that seems so simple but there are a few things that can go wrong. I have tried panna cotta many, many times and at one stage my husband said "no more!". But I can say that this is my ultimate recipe, it all comes down to ratio of liquid to gelatine to give perfect wobble and good set. If you feel uncomfortable about demoulding or, just want less work at the end, serve in glasses or in pretty tea cups. A good one for a dinner party as you can make ahead of time (even the night before).

300ml (10 fluid oz) FairTrade coconut cream*
300ml (10 fluid oz) milk
⅓ cup unrefined FairTrade unrefined sugar
3 sheets gelatine*

TO SERVE
1 fresh pineapple
1 pawpaw
6 passionfruit
Edible flowers (optional) (I used Tigers Eye violas.)

Makes: 6 (½ cup moulds)
Time: Easy as / takes time to set – at least 5 hours or overnight

* If you're not partial to coconut, use 300ml regular cream instead of coconut cream and add an extra tablespoon of sugar to make up for the sweetness from the coconut cream.

*I find gelatine sheets give a much silkier set than powdered gelatine. Powdered gelatine is quite strong. If you can't source gelatine sheets, use three LEVEL teaspoons of powdered gelatine instead.

Combine the cream, milk and sugar in a medium saucepan and warm over a medium heat for about 2 minutes or until the sugar dissolves. Do not boil – the mixture can't be too hot when you add the gelatine or it won't set correctly. Remove from heat. Soften the gelatine sheets in a little warm water in a bowl. Remove and squeeze out excess water. Add to warm milk mixture and stir with a whisk until dissolved. You want to do this with care – again, if it hasn't dissolved correctly it won't set. Strain through a sieve to ensure there are no pieces of gelatine. Cool to room temperature. Put your 6 ramekins (I use metal dariole moulds) onto a small tray for easy transportation to the fridge. Pour mixture into ramekins and refrigerate until set, this takes around 5 hours. You can make these a day ahead.

For the salsa: Cut the skin from the pineapple. Cut into quarters and remove the tough inner core. Slice into thin strips and then dice. For the pawpaw, cut skin off and remove the cheeks of the pawpaw. Cut into the same size dice as the pineapple. Combine in a bowl and set aside.

To serve: To easily demould panna cotta, take a paring knife and run around the rim of the panna cotta. Don't go too far in or you will have knife marks around the circumference. One at a time, dip the moulds into warm water, being careful not to get the panna cotta wet, for about 30 seconds. When you lift the mould out, touch the base with your fingers, it should not be cold – with a metal mould it's easy to test temperature. (Don't leave them sitting in the water however, or they will melt). Place a plate in the centre of the mould and invert, holding both plate and mould together, give it one firm shake. Gently lift mould off. If stuck, dip in warm water again and repeat process. Do this process with remaining panna cotta.

Once all demoulded, spoon over some of the salsa. Scoop out the flesh of a passionfruit per plate. Garnish with edible flowers if using.

LEMON CURD 'ETON MESS'

If you want an easy dessert to put together for a dinner party, this is it! You can use store-bought meringue and lemon curd, or you can make your own – it really can be simple or a little more "homemade" – it's completely up to you. I love the combination of texture, freshness, tart and sweetness in this dessert.

5 meringues
10 tablespoons thick Greek yoghurt
    (I used a vanilla bean flavoured one,
    or you can use whipped cream)
10 tablespoons lemon curd (see my recipe
    page 146)
5 scoops vanilla ice cream
1 punnet fresh raspberries

Serves: 5   Time: Easy as

Crumble the meringues into the bottom of the glass, reserving a little bit to garnish. Top with a tablespoon of yoghurt and lemon curd into each glass. Top with a scoop of ice cream followed by another tablespoon of yoghurt and lemon curd. Garnish with raspberries and crumble over remaining meringues. Serve immediately.

CHOCOLATE POTS

Chocolate pots are a really simple dessert which can be made ahead of time and chilled. They are so easy to put together and require hardly any cooking, just the warming of the cream, a little mixing and slicing, so it's a great dessert for beginner cooks. You can change the liquor to a raspberry one and top with fresh raspberries or add a little rum if you want, add some hazelnut liquor and garnish with chopped roasted hazelnuts, or if you want to keep it alcohol free, you could add a little coffee to really bring out the flavour of the chocolate. I love the combination of orange and chocolate. If you don't have Cointreau on hand, you can just buy a little 50ml mini bar bottle for this dessert. This is a really rich and intense dessert so a little goes a long way. I made six with this recipe, but you could easily get 8 portions. Serve in long shot glasses with teaspoons as an option too for more petite portions.

300ml (10 fluid oz) cream
¼ cup FairTrade unrefined sugar
300g (10oz) 70% FairTrade chocolate
1 tablespoon butter
1 tablespoon (or a little more to taste if you
    like) of orange liquor – Cointreau

TO SERVE
200ml (7 fl oz) cream
1 tablespoon icing sugar
4 oranges, skin and pith peeled and thinly
    sliced

Serves 6–8
Time: Easy as to make / allow 1 hour
setting time

Warm the cream and sugar in a medium size pot until almost at a boiling point, then remove and take off the heat. Add the chocolate and the butter to the cream and let it sit for 2 minutes. Whisk to combine the chocolate and the cream mixture together, then mix in the orange liquor. Pour evenly between serving glasses and chill for at least an hour.

Note: if you get a few marks around the glass with the chocolate, it's far easier to wipe it off now than when it's set. I wipe away the chocolate spills and then I always run a paper towel around the inside and outside of the glasses to ensure they are nice and clean for presentation.

Whip the remaining cream and fold through the icing sugar. When ready to serve, add a few slices of oranges to the glass followed by a dollop or quenelle of cream on top.

RASPBERRY MOUSSE CAKE

This is my real show stopper dessert and has so many amazing textures and flavours. It does require a lot of work including making the moulds. To make the moulds I cut long strips of acetate (available from stationery stores) three layers thick to hold its shape holding it in place with tape. The moulds I made were 4cm circle x 5cm high. You can use just one layer of acetate inside a presentation ring if you prefer – that is easier, but more expensive to buy the rings.

BASES
5 x gingernut biscuits
4 tablespoons melted butter

RASPBERRY MOUSSE FILLING
300g (10oz) fresh or frozen raspberries
  (thawed)
165ml (5.8oz) milk
3 free range egg yolks
85g (3oz) caster sugar
2 teaspoons powdered gelatine
1 tablespoon raspberry liqueur
165ml (5.8oz) thickened cream
2 teaspoons icing sugar

RASPBERRY JELLY TOPS
75ml (2.6oz) water
60ml (2oz) raspberry liqueur
1 teaspoon powdered gelatine

ALMOND PRALINE
100g (7oz) FairTrade unrefined sugar
1 tablespoon water
80g (3oz) blanched almonds

RASPBERRY COULIS
125g (1 cup/4.4oz) raspberries
¼ cup FairTrade unrefined sugar
1 teaspoon lemon juice

TO SERVE
8 fresh raspberries
Salted brittle caramel chocolate shards
Caramel ice cream (store-bought or see
  my recipe on my website)

Makes: 8
Time: Very time consuming

Bases: Crush the biscuits to fine crumbs. Mix with the melted butter and press into the base of the moulds with the back of a teaspoon. Make sure it's well pressed in especially to the edges so the mousse doesn't run out when you add that next layer.

Mousse filling: Blend raspberries until smooth. Push through a sieve to remove seeds. Set aside 60ml (2oz) of the raspberry liquid for the jelly – the rest is for the mousse. Heat milk over a medium heat until hot but not boiling. Remove from heat and set aside. Whisk yolks and sugar until smooth. Gradually whisk in hot milk then return to same saucepan, stirring over a low heat until mixture coats the back of a spoon and forms a smooth custard. Remove from heat. Sprinkle gelatine into 75ml (2.5oz) of boiling water. Stir until completely dissolved. Stir into custard with liqueur and remaining puree. Place in the fridge to cool (mixture has to cool otherwise when you add the whipped cream, the cream will melt). Beat cream and icing sugar with an electric mixer until soft peaks form. Fold cream into cooled raspberry custard. Divide mixture on top of the biscuit bases. Refrigerate for 3 hours or overnight.

Raspberry jelly top: Stir water, liqueur and reserved 60ml (2oz) of raspberry puree in a small saucepan over a medium/high heat until hot. Sprinkle in gelatine and whisk until completely dissolved. Cool completely to room temperature then pour over the mousse in the moulds (mousse must be set or semi-set so the layers sit on top of each other) refrigerate for 2 hours or overnight.

Almond praline: Line a tray with baking paper. Stir sugar and water in a small saucepan over low heat until sugar dissolves then cook without stirring until it turns dark golden. Quickly stir in the almonds to coat evenly then pour onto prepared tray. Allow to set and cool. Break up and add to a food processor and pulse to form coarse crumbs. Put into an airtight container. (Leftover praline stores well in the freezer)

Raspberry coulis: Bring the raspberries and sugar to the boil. Simmer, stirring occasionally, for about 15 minutes until it thickens slightly. Strain and press through a sieve to remove seeds. Stir in the lemon juice. Put into a squeeze bottle to make the line on the plate. I serve extra coulis on the side so people can help themselves.

To serve: Squeeze out a line of coulis onto each plate. Remove the raspberry mousse cakes from the mould by cutting and peeling off acetate and place on top of the coulis to one side. Place a fresh raspberry in the centre. Stab in a chocolate shard. Put a pile of the praline to the side with a scoop of ice cream on top.

MINI PAVLOVAS WITH SAFFRON STRAWBERRIES AND CREAM

A pavlova is crispy on the outside and soft, chewy and marshmallow like on the inside, compared to a meringue that is crisp and dry all the way through. That little addition of salt and cornflour stabilises the egg white helping to form that good shape and volume and the vinegar helps to give it that soft centre. I always use unrefined sugar for everything, except pavlovas! You need to use a fine sugar, castor sugar as it gives the best results when mixing with the egg whites as the sugar needs to be fully dissolved into the egg.

4 free range egg whites (preferably not
   fresh)
Pinch salt
1 cup castor sugar (200g/7oz)
1 teaspoon white vinegar
1 teaspoon cornflour

TO SERVE

1 cup cream
2 tablespoons icing sugar
1 teaspoon vanilla paste
2 punnets (250g each) strawberries
1 punnet (200g) raspberries
5 tablespoons saffron syrup (recipe below)
Edible flowers – I used black violas

Serves: 8
Time: Takes time

Preheat oven to 150°C (300°F) and prepare two baking trays and line with baking paper.

In a stand mixer (or by hand) whisk the egg whites with a pinch of salt until soft peaks form. Slowly add the castor sugar a spoonful at a time making sure that it has incorporated well with each addition. Once the sugar is added, I turn the mixer up and whisk for around 7 minutes. After that time, check to see if the mixture is ready by rubbing a little of the egg white between your fingers. You shouldn't be able to feel any grains from the sugar. If you can, continue to mix until you can't. Mix in the cornflour and vinegar.

Spoon out onto the prepared trays into 8 portions. They spread a little so space them out well. Smooth the pavlovas with the back of a metal spoon to give a nice finish. Bake for 30–35 minutes or until crisp. Turn the oven off and leave the door ajar with the pavlova inside the oven until the oven goes cold.

Whip the cream until it is soft. Fold through the icing sugar and vanilla paste. Set aside. Hull and quarter the strawberries and combine in a bowl with 2 tablespoons of the saffron syrup. Top each pavlova with a dollop of cream and the strawberries. Dot over the raspberries and garnish with editable flowers. Spoon remaining syrup around the plate.

SAFFRON SYRUP

I love the use of ingredients in an unusual way – if it works! And saffron syrup really does! You really get the taste of saffron, it doesn't get lost. Fold syrup through yoghurt and then spoon a dollop over ice cream or add a few drops to a glass of sparkling wine.

1 good pinch saffron
1 cup FairTrade unrefined sugar
1 cup water

Makes: 1 cup
Time: Easy as

In a small frying pan over a medium/high heat, toast the saffron for a minute to release its flavour. Add to a ¼ cup of hot water and set aside to steep. In a small pot, warm the sugar and water over a medium/high heat stirring occasional to dissolve the sugar. Once the sugar has dissolved, add the saffron and bring to the boil, and cook for around 5 minutes or until the syrup has thickened slightly. Remove and store in an airtight container or jar in the fridge. Will keep in the fridge for a few months.

CHOCOLATE MOUSSE CAKE

This is my ultimate chocolate dessert! It has a fudge cake base and a fluffy, indulgent mousse topping, seriously good! It is perfect for a dinner party as it serves 12 people and can be made the day before. Serve it with some fresh berries or in winter when fresh berries are not available, you could make a coulis from frozen berries (recipe for coulis on page 166). I don't know what else to say ... this is just perfection to me!

FOR THE CAKE

150g (5.3oz) butter,
150g (5.3oz) real trade chocolate,
   I used 70%
5 free range eggs, separated
150g (5.4oz) FairTrade unrefined sugar
1 teaspoon vanilla paste or extract

FOR THE MOUSSE

200g (7oz) real trade chocolate, I used 50%
30g (1oz) butter
3 free range eggs, separated
300ml (½ pint) cream

TO SERVE

¼ cup FairTrade cocoa powder
300ml (½ pint) cream
2 tablespoons icing sugar
Fresh berries – raspberries or blueberries

Serves: 12
Time: Takes time

Preheat the oven to 180°C (350°F). Grease and line a 21cm (8 inch) springform cake tin.

Put the chocolate and butter in a metal or glass bowl and place over a pot of simmering water. Let it melt and when it looks like there are only a few bits left, stir well with a wooden spoon. If it is all fully melted, remove from heat. Allow to cool to room temperature so that the chocolate doesn't harden when the egg is added.

Whisk the egg whites with a pinch of salt until soft peaks form. Divide the sugar in half, half to use for the egg whites and the other half to use in the yolks. Add half of the sugar to the beaten egg whites and mix well until really thick and glossy, set aside for now.

In another bowl, beat the egg yolks with the remaining sugar until pale and thick. Fold the melted chocolate into the pale yolk mixture, then fold gently through the egg whites with a large metal spoon being careful not to beat the air out of the egg white. Gently pour into the prepared cake tin and bake for 40–50 minutes, or until a skewer poked into the centre comes out clean. Leave the cake to cool in the tin. Take a clean dry tea towel and press down on the centre of the cake to form an indentation for the mousse filling. I like to leave an edge around the cake (like a pizza), I put the cake in the freezer to cool while I make the mousse (put in the fridge if you're not a fast worker so the cake cools but doesn't freeze).

For the mousse, melt the chocolate and butter in a bowl over a pot as before, then remove from the heat and leave to cool to room temperature again. Whisk the egg whites in a clean, dry bowl until soft peaks form and set aside. Whip the cream until it is thick, not too soft. Set aside. Beat the egg yolks into the cooled chocolate, one at a time whisking well with each addition. Fold the cream and egg whites into the chocolate bit by bit. You want to keep as much of the volume from the cream and the egg whites but if you don't mix it completely; you will get white through the mousse if it isn't incorporated properly. Spread the mousse over the cooled cake. Put into the fridge until set, at least 2 hours.

To serve, whip cream until soft peaks form and fold through the icing sugar. Before you remove the cake from the tin, dust with cocoa powder. Cut the cake in half and then into quarters. Cut each quarter into thirds. To plate, serve a wedge of cake on the plate with a quenelle (or dollop) of cream and some berries on the side.

Drinks

I love nothing more than a good cocktail – the flavour combinations are just as pleasing as food when each ingredient is carefully and thoughtfully selected – and with that boozy hit...bonus! One thing I always do when planning a holiday, especially to new cities, is research places to eat at and cocktail bars to visit. Quite often my husband and I, on a date night, will eat out at a cheap but cheerful noodle house, spending only a small amount each per main and then spend double, even triple that, afterwards on one drink and maybe desserts, at a posh eatery. So fun! I prefer long and tall drinks I can take my time sipping on. A reward on a productive day, sunny weather makes it all the more enjoyable!

In this chapter I have included some of our favourite tipples, not all alcoholic. My lemonade is such a hit in our house and can also be made with lime or grapefruit for a change depending on what's available. And juicing became a way of getting raw vegetables into our toddler's diet – such a fresh and healthy idea, and if you visit markets like we do, you can pick up all the fruit you need at a steal!

SIMPLE SYRUP

A simple syrup is just that, simple, and is the sweetener base for cocktails. Because it's a syrup it blends so well into drinks. The general rule of thumb is "one to one" (ie ½ cup sugar to ½ cup water etc). You can use all different sugars – palm sugar for Asian cocktails or coconut sugar for coconut drinks. It's up to you what sugar you want to use.

1 cup FairTrade unrefined sugar
1 cup water

Makes: 1 cup   Time: Easy as

In a small pot warm the sugar and water over a medium/high heat, stirring occasionally until the sugar dissolves. Pour into a glass jar. You can store any leftovers in the fridge in the jar. In the summer, when we have cocktails, I usually make up a big batch of this every 2 weeks for an easy grab and chilled syrup waiting to use.

THAI 'MOJITO'

My all-time favourite cocktail ... with an Asian twist! Perfect for serving at an Asian inspired dinner party.

15ml (½ oz) lime juice
15ml (½ oz) palm sugar simple syrup
60ml (2oz) white rum
about ½ cup ginger beer (depending on
    your glass size)

TO SERVE
A few sprigs of fresh herbs, I used Thai
    basil, Vietnamese mint and common
    mint
Kaffir lime, sliced

Serves: 1   Time: easy as

In a jar shake together the lime juice, palm sugar simple syrup and white rum. Fill a glass with ice and pour over the rum mixture. Top with ginger beer and stir with a straw. Garnish with herbs and lime slices. Stir a little to combine.

Note: I leave my herbs whole, I hate getting a mojito at a bar and they have chopped the mint and it gets stuck in the straw and gets stuck in my teeth. I 'clap' the herbs between my hands to release the aromas and flavours.

WHISKY SOUR

One thing we always have in our house is a single malt collection. This is my version of my husband's favourite cocktail.

60ml (2oz) single malt whisky
20ml (0.7oz) simple syrup
15ml (½ oz) lemon juice
15ml (½ oz) egg white
a dash of Orange Bitters

Serves: 1   Time: Easy as

In a shaker (or large jar) with a few ice cubes, combine all of the ingredients by shaking vigorously for a minute. Pour over a glass filled with ice.

Note: If you want more "foam" you can quickly pulse the ingredients in a blender to get it super frothy. And if it's too sour and strong (for people like me) you can top with fresh orange juice.

VODKA WATERMELON COCKTAIL

One thing we used to do at parties in my university days was to slowly feed vodka into a whole watermelon then slice it up and serve it. This was based on that concoction with a few extra ingredients to make it super summery. This cocktail is girly and perfectly pink, I just love the natural colour from watermelon! You can of course leave out the vodka entirely if you want a delicious and refreshing drink for the entire family.

1 cup chopped, deseeded watermelon
1 cup coconut water (or you could use pink
grapefruit or cranberry juice)
1 tablespoon lime juice
15ml simple syrup (depending on how
sweet your watermelon is)
60ml vodka
Mint to serve

Serves: 2
Time: Easy as

In a blender, blend the watermelon, coconut water and lime juice. Taste and see if you need to add the simple syrup. I did, and just that little bit of sugar gave everything a lift and enhanced all the flavours. Stir in the vodka. Pour over ice filled glasses. Garnish with mint.

LEMONADE CORDIAL

One of the best things about our house is the huge lemon tree and the fruit that it supplies me with all year round. One thing I like to make a few times a year is homemade lemonade. It's such an easy recipe! And it's adaptable – I've switched the lemon juice for grapefruit juice before and it was really delicious. This recipe also freezes well.

1 cup water
1 cup FairTrade unrefined sugar
1 cup fresh lemon juice

TO SERVE
Water, sparkling or even club soda to
dilute
Lemon slices
Mint (optional)

Makes: 2 cups
Time: Easy as

In a medium sized saucepan, mix the sugar and water together, stirring with a wooden spoon. Over a medium heat, warm the syrup until the sugar dissolves. Remove from the heat and stir in the lemon juice. Cool completely and chill. To serve, pour a little syrup into ice filled glasses and top with water or soda (the amount of syrup depends on your taste, if you like it sweeter, add more) garnish with lemon slices.

FRESH JUICE

This is hardly a recipe, but more of an idea. I bought a juicer when my youngest son decided one day that he didn't want to eat vegetables, when only a few weeks before he was happily eating raw capsicum, celery and cucumber sticks. When I started juicing, it was my way of ensuring that he was getting the vegetables he needed and by adding apples, it sweetened the juice and he was none the wiser. Because our kids were only allowed milk or water, juice, no matter what the flavour – was a treat. The top of the range juicers are really expensive, but they do a good job at getting all of the nutrients out of the fruits and vegetable. Ours is a middle of the range one, but my mother-in-law's is so good, the pulp leftover from the juice is almost dry, and apparently that's how you can tell if it's good. Judy (my mother-in-law) also told me once to consume the juice that you have made within 30 minutes of juicing to get the most goodness from the freshly pressed juice. Juicing is such a good way of adding vegetables and fruits to your daily diet. You can use whatever fruits and vegetables you like and a squeeze of lemon or lime or a little ginger really lifts the flavours and makes everything taste better! Vegetable markets are a great place to source weekly juicing items cheaply if you don't grow them yourself.

1 orange
2 large carrots
½ celery stalk (celery is VERY strong in
    fresh juice)
5 large Swiss Chard leaves
6 apples
Squeeze lime
Mint to garnish

Juice everything in a juicer. Leave it to settle for a minute then I scrape off the foamy bit on top. Serve in glasses topped up with ice and garnish with mint.

Serves: 3   Time: Easy as

BLUEBERRY AND LSA SMOOTHIE

If you're not much of a breakfast person or you like to eat on the run, this is the perfect morning start for you! I'm not very adventurous when it comes to smoothies in terms of branching out, this is the only smoothie that I ever make because it's delicious! Blueberries are so good for you – out of season when fresh are hard to source, frozen ones are a good staple to keep handy in the freezer. And LSA (linseed – or flaxseed, sunflower seed and almonds) is a super food combo that gives you fibre and essential fatty acids. I buy it already ground in an organic brand, that is available by the packet – so convenient and ready to use on those busy weekday mornings.

1 cup blueberries
1 large FairTrade banana
1 teaspoon runny honey
1 teaspoon bee pollen (optional)
2 tablespoons LSA
2 tablespoons probiotic yoghurt
1 cup milk

Blend everything in a blender. Serve over ice if using fresh fruit, otherwise if your blueberries or banana have been frozen, it should be cold enough.

Serves: 2   Time: Easy as

PANTRY

This list includes items in my book that might be unusual or hard to source. I have tried to keep my book accessible giving alternatives where possible, but some items might be harder to source depending on where you live. If I find some ingredients hard to source, I search for the items online and usually find an online store in my country that can deliver to my door.

0

00 flour – for pasta and pizza base making this can be bought online from mediterranean food stores. Regular all-purpose flour can be used if 00 flour can't be sourced.

B

Black sesame seeds – are available from Asian supermarkets.

C

Chillies – I use long red chillies when in season. Alternatively I use a pinch of dried chilli flakes or chilli paste (from the spice section of the supermarket) Coconut chips – I buy these online. Corn tortillas – corn are better than flour ones and are available online. Chocolate – for real trade single origin chocolate search online. For the chocolate pearls used on my chocolate cake, try speciality stores.

E

Edible flowers – I grow my own, that way I know they are chemical-free. Most garden stores sell edible flowers and seeds. I let mine go to seed so that the following year flowers pop up again in the same spot (and quite often in other places too!).

F

Fair Trade – Fair Trade products can be sourced at most supermarkets as well as organic and whole food stores.

G

Grains – farrow, couscous, and quinoa grains are available from good organic product stores.

L

Limes – out of season, imported limes can be very expensive. So during that time, I used ready-squeezed lime juice in a bottle.
LSA – ground LSA (linseed, sunflower and almonds) I buy from good organic product stores.

M

Masa flour – a flour for making tortillas
Microgreens – these are available at specialty supermarkets. You can also buy seeds online and grow your own. They are really easy to grow and a lot cheaper.
Mung Beans – these are also known as mung bean sprouts and can be found in the chiller section of the produce (or vegetable) section of the supermarket. They are inexpensive and great in salads and Asian dishes.
Mushrooms – The more unusual mushrooms like oyster, shitake and needles can be found at most good supermarkets and farmers' markets.

O

Organic – organic produce is used in all my recipes.

P

Pasta – for pasta shapes, such as alphabet pasta, try online sources.

S

Seeds – I always have an array of seeds and nuts on hand in my pantry. Pine nuts are expensive so I like to use things like sunflower seeds which are cheap to balance out our food budget. I roast seeds in the oven – you get a much better flavour in the oven than dry roasting them in a pan.
Seeds for growing – it is fun to try heirloom varieties.
Salmon – try to source natural wood smoked salmon.
Saffron – saffron can be found in the spice section of the supermarket.

V

Vanilla paste might be a little harder to source than vanilla beans (vanilla beans are usually in the spice section of the supermarket).

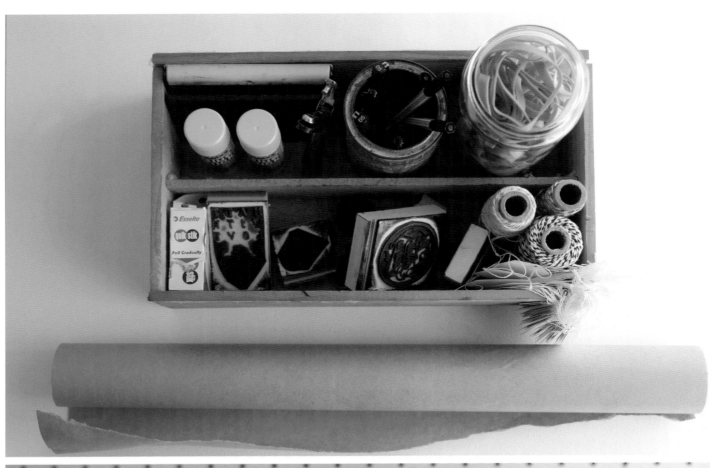

LABELLING

I always have people ask me on social media how I label all my jars, and because my labels are throughout the book, I thought I'd add a little 'how to' page. It's a great way of finishing and making things like preserves look pretty and personal, perfect for gift giving. But it doesn't stop there for me, I am label obsessed and anyone who has been to my house knows my jars! Everything goes into glass jars and gets a brown paper label, from spices to flour, teas to sugar.

JARS

We recycle glass jars and soak the labels off. Eucalyptus oil (available from Health food stores and pharmacies) is really good for removing labels that have that extra stubborn glue on them. Because we harvest a lot of honey, we never quite have enough recycled jars, so we buy extras.

RUBBER STAMPS

If you are labelling lots of the same thing, like our honey, it might be a good idea to get a rubber stamp made. Rubber stamp makers can turn anything into a stamp, I have even had our name and address made in my own hand writing into a stamp to stamp onto the back of envelopes for hand written letters. The honey stamp, made with love stamp and the leaf stamp that has been used in this book I designed in photoshop (in the size that I wanted the stamp) and then I sent the JPEG file to the stamp maker – or you can hand write something and take a clear sharp photo of the design and send that in. I chose 'self-stamping' stamps and bought an ink pad from a stationery store. One thing to keep in mind if you are getting a self-stamping one made is to make it no bigger than the ink pad (I have quite a large ink pad)

To make a hand written brown paper label, you will need (and all available from any stationery store):

- Brown craft paper – sometimes found in stationery stores by postage items like the envelopes and bubble wrap
- glue stick –use a non–toxic one
- black ink pen (I use a 0.5 black ink pen)
- Scissors
- Jumbo rubber bands
- Optional: white swing tags

How to write a label: I usually always make a circle label as if it's a bit wonky, it still looks good. Depending on the size of the jar will depend on what size your label will be.

1. Write the name of the thing you are labelling ie: raspberry jam
2. I always draw a laurel wreath around, I have done for years now, I guess it's just a signature thing I do; two simple branches that form a 'U' shape around the word.
3. Then I draw a circle around it all, slightly off shape is good. Then I make the circle thicker and heavier than the writing and laurel wreath.
4. Cut the label out with scissors leaving a slight gap around the circle .
5. Glue to the jar with a glue stick. Glue sticks hold the label onto the glass really well. Soaking in water easily removes it later.
6. If you are going to top the jar with a cover, you can do this with a square of fabric, but I usually do this with brown paper. Cut a square bigger than the lid. I had my *The Forest Cantina*' logo made into a 5cm circle stamp so that it can be stamped onto the brown paper tops and fit the circumference of most standard jar lids, so I always stamp the top of the paper cover to finish it off. Or sometimes I stamp the top with my leaf stamp. I then secure it with a thick rubber band.
7. I use swing tags to give details to the jars. I will add things like the date it was made, or if I have labelled the jar using my 'made with love' stamp, I will use the white swing tag to say what the contents are.

And that's it! Hope you enjoy labelling as much as I do!

GRATITUDE

"By doing what you love, you inspire and awaken the hearts of others". I am so thankful that I was given the opportunity to share my love of food and photography through this book. But I was only able to achieve it because of the layers of help and support of some very special people. The process of this book would not have been possible without family, friends, sponsors and supporters. Aary, Jah and Leo. Firstly a huge thanks to my husband Aaron, for your constant faith in my talent even when I had doubt. He is an incredibly hard worker who has supported us financially for years now because I choose to be a stay at home mum. I'm so grateful for all the things he made for this book, and all the time he put into getting things right for "his toughest client". We are ying and yang, a complementary balance; I hit the jackpot when I met you! My boys, Jah and Leo – you are the purpose for all I do, you bring me so much joy and smiles daily ... I would not be half the person I am today if I was not a mum and I feel so blessed that the two of you are in my life. There are certain dishes that I connect to my childhood – I hope there are things in this book that will forever remind you of me or a moment in time where we shared it together as a family. My three, I love you so much! X

To my family, I cannot even begin to explain how much I appreciate the support from my parents. Every week Mum and Dad would come and pick up Leo during the day, sometimes picking up Jah from school. Some days it would be from 9:30am–3:30pm, but more than often, the kids would be returned, bathed, fed and in their PJ's ready for bed later at night. It's the behind the scenes stuff like this that really is the heart of how a project on this scale gets done. Mum and Dad, thank you for always putting family first, thank you for the support that comes with no strings attached. For giving me your time and doing it because you sincerely want to. I know I am very blessed to have the parents that I do. Much love also to my two brothers Rich and Mike. Rich and Zea, because you live so close to us you probably ate 90% of the food in this cookbook and helped contribute to our (gigantic) food bill. It's awesome to have that support and spend all that time with you. Love to you both. To my Grandparents. Grandad – you are one of the biggest loves of my life. Right from the very beginning of life I always had a connection with you – you had a feeling of pure love around you that always made me feel calm and happy. It is so sad that you are not here to see the completion of this book, it actually breaks my heart. You will always have a mark on my life and I think about you almost every day. Gran, you also are not here to see this book in the flesh. But throughout much of the making of the book I felt your presence; I felt that you were there with me and watching me cook. Your food will always be one of my greatest memories I have. You were a grandmother who always wore an apron, who grew her own, preserved, baked, and made each and everything you did with love and care. I'm sure you will be proud to see some of your recipes in my book, just as I am so proud to include them in my collection.

Friends and extended family. A special thanks to all my extended family and friends, the people who make our lives so rich and fun. The people who supported me right from the very beginning. For your encouragement and for your belief in me before I even knew something existed. To those of you who encouraged me to blog and share my love of food. That was the very first push that eventuated in this huge journey in my life. Much love to you all.

AND THANKS

To the friends of *The Forest Cantina* – to people I have connected with who have made such a mark on this book. People like Alana at Fancy: New Zealand design blog for featuring me on your gorgeous site. It was through that post that I was discovered from the publishing company to write this book. For that I will always be truly grateful. Thanks to Ben and Elise for the lifestyle photography – honestly you guys are so insanely talented and it's been such a pleasure working with you both. Thank you for being perfectionists with such a wonderful eyes for the details. I knew when I commissioned you both that you would exceed my expectations, and you have. Josiah at Firetale films. Thank you for putting together the film to go with this book. It really added an emotion to the process that only film can do. I am thankful to have found you to work with, it's been a real pleasure and you had made me feel at ease right from the beginning. To Felicity from Wundaire Ceramics. I am so lucky that we connected and found each other online which brought us together to collaborate. Your ceramics are truly beautiful and I've loved using your works in this book and at the dinner. You have made almost 100 pieces for me, all by hand, and I love each and every one of them. I appreciate all the time you have put into your craft for me. To Joan Tarrago for the logo. You are the one person who contributed to this book who lived so far away, in Barcelona. You are such a wonderful person to work with and you really captured *The Forest Cantina* in your design so perfectly. I hope one day our paths can cross in real life. To Mindy from Twig and Arrow for the beautiful florals you created for the table at the dinner I hosted, it looked STUNNING and you nailed the brief! You are such a joy and talented person to work with. To Wellington Chocolate factory for all the FairTrade chocolate used in this book and also for letting me use your gorgeous space for the dinner, thank you Rochelle! Your passion for what you do is truly inspiring and also incredibly infectious. I have so much respect for what you do. To Morv at Antipodes water, for seeing something in me right from the start, before I even had belief in what I was doing and for all your support sharing my work online and in the magazines, and of course, for all the cases of water! AND for finding a wine sponsor for me! You are the loveliest person to work with and I look forward to exciting things together in the future with you and Antipodes. To Alice Lines from Homestyle Magazine for your styling help with the kitchen shoot, for all the time you put into sourcing amazing things for me and also introducing me to some wonderfully talented people. I love how since then we have made it a priority to catch up when in each other's cities. Finding new friends and connections via social media as well as working with some super talented people has been a real blessing this year.

Sponsors. HUGE thank you to these amazing people and companies for giving me your products and services for the book. Wellington Chocolate Factory for the chocolate. Pizza Pomodoro, Wellington. Pop Roc Parties: everything from drink dispensers, straws to string. Antipodes Water Company for all the water! Kathryn Leah Payne for the leather plant holders in my kitchen. Regal King Salmon for the salmon. Lot Eight for the olive oil. Tuatara Brewing Company for the beer. Huia Wine's for the wine. Kowtow Clothing for the clothing and Stem Distribution Ltd for organizing clothing for the shoots from Brixton and Poler. Josh at Chop Hairdressing for doing mine and Jahs' hair for the photoshoots. Father Rabbit for the props on loan for the book and styling, and for also reaching out and being the first person to say you wanted to stock my book. Citta Design for the glassware (on loan for the dinner). To Paperplane and Let Liv for loaning things from your stores for the kitchen shoot also. Thank you so much everyone!

Supporters. Of course a huge thank you to New Holland Publishing for publishing me, for making this all happen and believing in my creative vision for this book and for allowing me to have this dream come true. Special shout out to Christine, for all the emails and support throughout this process. To Capital Magazine, who I write a food column for, that experience really has been truly helpful with my writing for this book, I will always be grateful for the opportunity I have with you. And lastly to all my friends, followers and the people I have met on Instagram and Facebook. It is through your encouragement and kind words that has really given me the confidence and courage to do what I do. I never would have been able to grow to the point of where I'm at now if it wasn't for all the kind and supportive words I get daily from you all. I will forever be grateful for your support.

Thanks and love, Unna x

thank
you
x

INDEX

First published in 2015 by New Holland Publishers Pty Ltd
London • Sydney • Auckland

The Chandlery Unit 009 50 Westminster Bridge Road London SE1 7QY United Kingdom
1/66 Gibbes Street Chatswood NSW 2067 Australia
5/39 Woodside Ave Northcote, Auckland 0627 New Zealand

www.newhollandpublishers.com

Managing Director: Fiona Schultz
Publisher: Christine Thomson
Project Editor: Holly Willsher
Designer: Lorena Susak
Production Director: Olga Dementiev
Printer: Toppan Leefung Printing Limited

10 9 8 7 6 5 4 3 2 1

Keep up with New Holland Publishers on Facebook
www.facebook.com/NewHollandPublishers